# How to Write Effective Business English

D0300580

# How to Write Effective Business English

## Excel at e-mail, social media and all your professional communications

FIONA TALBOT

**KoganPage**

LONDON PHILADELPHIA NEW DELHI

First published in Great Britain and the United States in 2016 by Kogan Page Limited

| 2nd Floor, 45 Gee Street | 1518 Walnut Street, Suite 1100 | 4737/23 Ansari Road |
| London EC1V 3RS | Philadelphia PA 19102 | Daryaganj |
| United Kingdom | USA | New Delhi 110002 |
| | | India |

© Fiona Talbot, 2016

The right of Fiona Talbot to be identified as the author of this work has been asserted by her in accordance with the Copyright, Designs and Patents Act 1988.

ISBN    978 0 7494 7555 0
E-ISBN 978 0 7494 7556 7

**British Library Cataloguing-in-Publication Data**

A CIP record for this book is available from the British Library.

**Library of Congress Control Number**
2015036203

Typeset by Amnet Systems
Print production managed by Jellyfish
Printed and bound by Ashford Colour Press Ltd.

*I would like to thank all of you – my family, readers, friends, clients, and my commissioning editors at Kogan Page, Julia Swales and Géraldine Collard – for your support and interest in the wonderful world of #wordpowerskills.*

*Special thanks go to my dear husband, Colin; to Alexander and Hannah-Maria, Johanna and Daren. It's with great joy that I also see the youngest members of the family, Jude and Dominique, taking delight in words. I dedicate this book to you all.*

# Contents

# Preface

*Don't just be enthusiastic in #socialmedia. It's passion, not management speak, that engages readers throughout all your corporate communications.* FIONA TALBOT

## Who is this book for?

If you are in business (or are preparing to enter the workplace) and you grasp the inescapable fact that the written word takes centre stage in business communication today, then this is the ideal business English primer for you. Its extensive task-based guidance provides a toolkit for developing the highly prized workplace skills that bosses need.

Increasingly, English is the language of choice in the information age, widely used on the web and in multinational gatherings. It may not be the predominant language of the group, but is the most likely to be understood by the majority – at least at a basic level – so becomes a powerful tool for communication and inclusion. In the age of social media, the English language has commercial global currency. It can give the power to reach out not just to English-speaking home markets but internationally too.

So this book is aimed equally at native and non-native English speakers (who are proficient to intermediate level and above). Whichever you are, you will uncover valuable tips on how to get your business English writing right on every level.

# Be effective by writing content of value

Effective writing is no longer just about traditional reports, presentations, letters and so on. Today, writing skills matter more than ever: in e-mail, instant messaging, infographics and social media – even in the fast-growing medium of video storytelling where meaningful captions and calls to action are key.

Today's need is for content of value. And content means every word you use in every business writing task you do. Everything should add up to make great corporate communication.

Bosses need people who can write well, grab attention for the right reasons, influence, persuade, reflect brand and values and enhance reputation... all in the shortest time.

And if you are a start-up operating from home, you too can have the same potential global reach as the large corporate. The rules of engagement involve writing to impress, sell messages, values, products or services, and create a following and brand reputation based on trust. These principles are the same for all.

# How does the book work?

The book will work for anyone who is a native English speaker or proficient in English to intermediate level and above.

It teaches my four-step Word Power Skills writing system which is now used worldwide. It's about:

- identifying the right messages at planning stage, communicating these clearly and interestingly so that people understand you – and want to read on;

- being professional and getting the results you and your readers need.

The book describes scenarios every office encounters and gives practical advice on how to write successfully. The real-life examples make great discussion points with bosses and colleagues – and you will be able to customize the tips for your every writing task.

The beauty of the system is that it works across traditional and emerging new channels.

This book is the first in a series of three. You can find out more about the Better Business English series on page 147.

## You may have to unlearn some things you learnt at school

Writing English for business today is unlikely to be the same as the writing you were taught at school or university. Apart from getting your punctuation and grammar right, the similarities often end there. With countries the world over facing a shortage of people with key communication skills, employers cry out for people who can impress, sell messages, values and brand, consistently and professionally.

## Get results!

Just take a look at my methods, focus on the elements that apply to your business writing and make sure they become an intrinsic part of your real-life performance.

Enjoy using word power as a free resource – indeed my clients find they buzz with it! Enjoy too the benefits of immediate results and sustainable improvements.

Good luck on your journey to success!

Fiona Talbot
TQI Word Power Skills
www.wordpowerskills.com

# Introduction

This book is an essential guide to keep with you, by your desk or on your travels. It provides a wealth of answers to help you impress and shine through effective business English writing for the modern workplace.

Look on it as your introduction to being the best! By the time you reach the end, you will be more confident and more competent in writing English.

As well as dealing with traditional writing, this book shows how writing for social media has turned the world of business writing inside out. It actually needs a whole new mind-set and an integrated approach to work.

This 'new kid on the block' relies on the written word – and is vying for centre stage. It's also making us reassess all corporate communication in its light. Responsive businesses will grasp the need to welcome its ascendancy; the complacent will fail to give it the attention it deserves. The only constant now is communicating professionally and credibly at all times – and the writing system you are shown throughout the book works across all tasks and every medium.

You will be developing a key transferable skill that employers welcome and that can open doors for your career, since English is the global business language of today.

# Chapter One
# Why are you writing?

## Who are your readers?

Throughout this book I use the terms readers, target readership, customers and audience interchangeably. A 'customer' can be a person who buys goods or services from a business, or can be a person you deal with in the course of your daily work. The term applies just as much to internal colleagues, suppliers, those in the public sector etc as it does to those who are external consumers.

### Your audience can be anyone and everyone

Where you know your target audience's profile, you have an immediate advantage. The digital age is all about customizing products and services to suit the individual customer. It works for communication too. By what means does your target readership like to receive messages? Are you able to match their needs and cultural expectations and engage their interest because you know their profile? It's great news if you can.

But there's something new happening as well. The potential global reach of your e-writing (which includes social media) is really exciting. The business that operates from home can have as loud a voice as the large corporate. Your messages may (perhaps unexpectedly) be forwarded on by others, even go viral. So every business message, personalized or not, had better be professional! Nothing should be open to misinterpretation or cause offence, even unintentionally.

Many practical examples and scenarios in this book relate to sales or customer pitches. Because we're all consumers in our private lives, we can relate to and understand these examples. What I would like to stress is that the concepts apply equally to every scenario in the list that follows. Think of lobbying; think of politics; think of charities; think of fundraising; think of promotions.

## What's the purpose of your writing?

People sometimes think of business writing as a 'soft' skill as opposed to the 'hard' skills of finance, law, IT etc. But I think this description is misleading. The label 'soft' can give the impression that business writing is an easy skill, which it certainly is not. Business writing can impact on the whole business cycle; it can win business, it can lose business and it can communicate the framework by which results can be achieved.

This is why, at the outset of my training workshops, I always take time to ask people why they actually write in their job and what outcomes they seek, individually and as teams. I ask clients to write down why they need to write in their businesses, and the following aspects of business writing always come top of the list:

- to inform or record;
- to cascade information;
- for compliance;
- to seek information;
- to write specifications;
- to achieve a standard;
- to write reports with recommendations;
- to persuade;
- to promote services.

Usually far lower on the list (and sometimes only when prompted by me, on the lines of 'Aren't there any other reasons?'), they record such things as:

- to engage interest and involve;
- to get the right results;
- to sell;
- to support customers;
- to improve life for customers;
- to create a following;
- to influence;
- to change things/innovate/disrupt;
- to enhance brand and reputation;
- to show our personality;
- to reflect our values;
- to eat, breathe and live our vision.

Notice how the most inspirational aspects of writing are the ones that are listed as an afterthought!

Why is this? Maybe companies need to focus more on how powerful business writing can be and how their employees need to think creatively about how best to harness this virtually free resource. Think about what writing really means for your company and which aspects of your business it covers.

**Activity:** Each time you write, first ask yourself:

1  Why am I writing?

2  What are my/my company's values and objectives?

3  Do I have a definite or outline profile for my target audience?

4  What are their values and needs?

5  How will I align my message(s)?

6  What style, vocabulary (and medium, where you have a choice) are likely to suit them best?

7  How can I project my company's 'personality' and create an opportunity to shine myself?

Your writing simply won't work if you don't first plan what you need to achieve!

# Readers take just a few seconds to judge your writing

The written word is unforgiving. When I read, I judge what I see written for what it is. If I am looking for products or services, what I see can be what I think I get. If it is your writing, I will judge both you as an individual and your company on the basis of how you expressed yourself at that point in time. That's how important writing is.

It's commercial folly that many written messages lead to confusion and misunderstanding – even when a company is writing in its native language. Poor writing can also lead to customer complaints. At the least, this complicates relations with customers – even if we manage to convert a complaint to a positive experience.

The worst scenarios are where customers walk away from the companies concerned, and tell others about the bad experience they have received or think they have received. That's the impact that ineffective writing can have. It becomes quite clear that if, as customers, we do not understand or like what supplier A is writing, we prefer to buy from supplier B, who cares enough about our needs to get the message right. And if this takes less time, so much the better.

## *No body language signals in writing*

When we communicate face to face, people around us attach importance to the signals given by our body language. These are said to account for 55 per cent of the impact we make when giving a talk. Our voice can account for perhaps 38 per cent – and our words just 7 per cent.

This is because, in face-to-face communication, unlike writing, we don't need to focus just on words. We can ask if we are not sure what is being said. We can look for clues from the speaker's facial expression or tone as to the gravity or levity of the subject matter. These will help our understanding and focus our attention (or not!).

But with writing now taking centre stage in today's workplace (think e-mail, instant messaging, social media), it's the words that are crucial. Unless the writer is there in front of you, time will elapse before you get answers to any questions you have. That is, if you have the time or inclination to ask questions. At the very least, it means that writers need to think twice, spellcheck – in fact, double-check – that their words are saying what they mean them to say.

# How formal or informal do you need to be?

Business writing is in a state of flux. One thing you will notice is that business writing in English is becoming increasingly diverse in style. Different styles may even coexist within the same company. It can be bewildering for reader and writer alike as I will show throughout the book. Generally speaking, the move in business English writing is not only towards more 'people' words, but also towards more informality, largely thanks to social media.

This can be a special challenge for some cultures. Asian cultures, for example, place great emphasis on hierarchy, where people of senior grades are treated with noticeably more deference and respect than those in junior grades. Informality can also be a challenge for nationalities where there is a distinction between a familiar and a formal form of the pronoun 'you'. Even Western cultures can do this; for example, French makes a distinction between *tu* (informal) and *vous* (formal). Such cultures can try to compensate for this lack of distinction by writing more elaborately for what they see as the 'formal you' as opposed to the 'informal you'. This doesn't necessarily work.

## Your checklist for action

- Recognize writing as a fundamental skill for you as an individual and for your business.
- Develop and improve your writing at every opportunity to impress, influence, and boost your career.
- Remember that English business writing – in its many forms – is your most common route to market. Be the best.

# Chapter Two
# Business writing for today

## Winning business through English

Years ago, it often took longer to do deals than it does today. The ritual involved initial telephone enquiries or formal letters of introduction, preliminary and follow-up meetings for two or more parties to 'sound each other out'.

Today the layer of detailed introductions and small talk has partly given way to addressing the real purpose: to drive business success.

There may be a gap between how you were taught to write English at school and how you need to write it for business. English for business today is very much about 'how to win business through English'.

## Academic writing compared with writing for business

These are two almost entirely different genres. Their goals are different and they require different approaches, which I will outline now.

### Academic writing requirements

Students are generally required to write structured essays, research papers and theses. These are largely marked on the basis of how well students have managed to access the right information, process this, show prose/composition skills and accuracy, and conform to a fairly standard presentation format. By and large, the structure involves a beginning (topic and purpose), a middle (evidence and argument, or thesis) and an end (conclusion). The words and tone used must be relevant for the world of academe. This can require a formal, objective, impersonal style and an extensive, specialized vocabulary can gain marks.

## Business writing requirements

In the workplace, you certainly need to know how to access the right information and process this when you write. You need to be accurate too. Some companies require you to follow a standard house style. But you may be allowed to make suggestions about how the house style could evolve, in view of changing business circumstances and customers' needs.

But there is one very interesting recent evolution in writing business English and it's probably due to the fact that attention spans are lessening, thanks to the I-want-it-now immediacy of the information age. There are fewer occasions now when business writing is seen to have the academic-style beginning, middle and end structure (other than in certain formal reports). You may need to develop skills that your teachers may not have taught you and that you may not have come across previously.

# Can you use 'I' when you write in business?

You may need to shed the rules of school writing when you enter the workplace. For example, time after time I hear people say, 'We were taught at school that we can't use "I" and "we" in the same sentence in a letter', or 'You can't write "I" in business; it must always be "we"'.

Many companies feel that a key driver of business success is empowerment of the individual. For them, it's about everyone being given the power and encouragement to make a difference within their organization. There may be 'no I in team' (I am using this management speak ironically here!) but to embrace the concept of 'I/me' can be crucial. And such companies may also encourage you to write 'we' (even within the same piece of writing), to demonstrate that each person is an integral part of the total company.

You will certainly find plenty of evidence from companies worldwide that you can use 'I' and 'we' within your sentences – but always research company culture first.

## Other things that you may wish to 'unlearn'

You may have been taught that you cannot begin a sentence with 'And' or 'But'. Actually you can – and many acclaimed writers do. For traditionalists, let me mention the famous English novelist Jane Austen as one example. I often begin sentences with these words throughout this series, as the style seems relevant for today. This is largely because e-writing is today's predominant business writing and its style is mostly halfway between conversation and formal writing. There is a knock-on effect on the way people write other documentation. This is not about 'dumbing down'; it's about expressing facts simply, in accessible writing that speaks to people.

It's true to say that if I had a specific customer or line manager who hated sentences beginning with 'And' or 'But', I wouldn't use that style with them. Similarly, if my publishers did not accept the style, I would avoid it – but they agree it's appropriate for standard business English writing. Naturally, it is essential to be reader-driven when you write. As I cannot have the advantage of knowing each of you, my readers, I will use a generic style.

But where you can, put out your antennae and tune in to what people don't like! There are always alternatives you can choose.

Here are some examples that regularly crop up in my training workshops. Where at all possible, people prefer to read:

'For this to work, you/we need to...' rather than 'It must be done.'

'Yes, I've done that' rather than 'Done.'

'Thank you for bringing this to our attention' rather than 'We note...'

'So that we can reach our targets, please could I have these figures tomorrow?' rather than 'I need these figures tomorrow.'

'We are really sorry we can't help (because...) rather than 'We cannot help.'

Can you see the pattern emerging? People tend not to like terseness and they like to be given reasons why things have to be done. Ask for assistance, and they are more likely to help!

I find it often helps to draw up two lists. One can be a list of 'Things to avoid' and includes any expressions or style that you know your boss doesn't like or that your readers have criticized. On the plus side, you can also draw up a list of 'Things that worked' and get in the habit of using these.

## Listen to readers' feedback

Do ask readers for feedback on your business English writing. You can learn so much. Companies who take the time to do so find that readers routinely comment that:

- they feel patronized by poorly written letters;
- they can feel insulted by writers' lack of attention to the right detail;
- they don't sense the 'human touch' in much of the language used in business writing;

- they can feel so angered by correspondence that, where they can do so, they will walk away from the business concerned;

- they dislike unnecessary jargon (words or expressions used by a particular profession or group that may be difficult for others to understand), over-complicated sentences and confusing use of words;

- they are offended when their personal details are incorrect.

Do re-read this list from time to time. Never lose sight of how readers may react. I will be dealing with all these aspects of writing in this book but will just highlight one of the most common now. It's this: what do you think the lack of the 'human touch' in writing could mean? Is it the fact that business writers actively avoid using 'people' words such as 'you' and 'we'? Let me demonstrate. A company writes to a client on the following lines:

---

Dear Sir

**Re: Policy XYZ**

It has come to the company's attention that the aforementioned policy that is about to expire has not yet been renewed. I enclose a renewal form, which you need to return within seven days, otherwise you will no longer be afforded cover.

Yours faithfully
John Smith

Smith and Co

Some companies still this use stilted, old-fashioned English and I cannot imagine why. Especially now, as we live in a world where customers increasingly expect to feel the personal touch – and to feel valued. So let's redesign the message, using people words and more modern English.

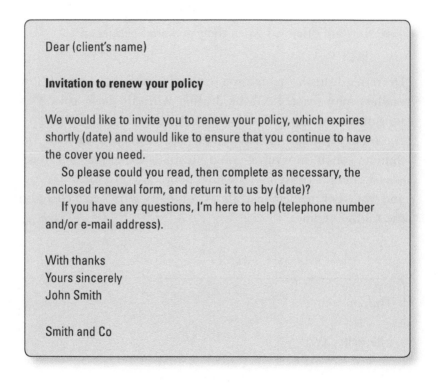

Dear (client's name)

**Invitation to renew your policy**

We would like to invite you to renew your policy, which expires shortly (date) and would like to ensure that you continue to have the cover you need.
  So please could you read, then complete as necessary, the enclosed renewal form, and return it to us by (date)?
  If you have any questions, I'm here to help (telephone number and/or e-mail address).

With thanks
Yours sincerely
John Smith

Smith and Co

As I write, I've just received a letter from my car insurers and it certainly ends with a human touch:

**Thank you**
Thank you again for insuring your car with us for another year and we wish you a safe year of driving.

Try to be personable through your writing. People do like it.

# Choosing the right style

More examples follow, showing how writers and readers alike can be confused by differing styles of written English within their own company.

1  Therefore, although obviously we cannot make any assessment about the matter in hand on this occasion, we will nevertheless take cognizance of the contents of your letter and will forthwith forward a copy thereof to the managing director who has the appropriate responsibility for investigating any issues raised.

2  Done.

3  Thanks loads.

The style in the first example is extremely formal English and quite old-fashioned in feel. You can see what I term barrier words: 'therefore', 'obviously', 'nevertheless' and 'forthwith'. They are all correct English, but they can make readers feel distanced. The majority of readers will probably view the writer as condescending towards an 'inferior' reader, rather than communicating with a valued customer.

The one word 'Done' in the second example is a common e-mail response these days, when someone has asked a question such as 'Have you completed this action?' Those who write the one-word reply usually feel they are very effective workers and communicators. What they don't see is the irritated face on the receiving end of the e-mail! The one-word reply is so often seen as plain rude. Just by adding three words and changing the reply to 'I have done that' you can make the writing seem less curt and more polite. As people comment on this in so many training workshops that I run, it's well worth a mention here.

The third example is informal in the extreme, yet you see it a lot in business today. It does convey goodwill, but many find it unprofessional and inappropriate for corporate communication.

Some writers say they are only that informal when writing for someone they really know. But the problem is, e-mails can so often continue in threads – and may be forwarded in time to external recipients too.

## CASE STUDY   Choosing the right style

One major supermarket chain issued a product recall. They had discovered that an axe they sold had a design fault. The head could become detached from the handle.

The retailer decided to ditch the old-fashioned approach to a Product Recall notice, which in the past might have started: 'A decision has been taken to recall (description of product) as it has been found to be faulty. Please return the product immediately for a refund... (full details of method...).'

Instead, they decided to refresh their style and the Product Recall notice included these words:

> Our (product details) axe would be fantastic apart from the fact that the head can become detached from the handle. Quite clearly, this is not on so we have decided that you need to know. Thankfully no one has been hurt. (They then go on to detail how customers can get a refund).

The recall ends with 'It goes without saying... we're very sorry indeed.'

What do you think of this approach? At first sight, many people quite like it. When they read on, they often change their mind, finding the style too light-hearted for a potentially highly dangerous scenario. And how does the retailer know that nobody has been hurt, just because they hadn't been notified before they posted the recall?

Effective business writing has to 'think ahead' for all sorts of possibilities – and adopt the right style for the situation as well as the audience.

You are likely to see contrasts in business English writing in your company. Do consider whether taking a middle course, a median between an overly formal or overly informal style, is going to work best, to avoid unnecessarily confusing styles.

# Ideal communication

It's hard to define ideal business communication but this summary is useful:

> Effective written communication is when the correct, concise, current message is sent out to the primary receiver(s), then onwards without distortion to further receivers to generate the required response.

Let me amplify. Sometimes we write to someone simply to inform them of something. They then remain the primary receiver. The only response we require is one that favours the way we have delivered the message (both on a personal and a company level).

Probably more often our aim when we write is to do more than simply inform. We're looking for the receiver(s) to like our style and to do something too. Our writing should influence them and actively enable this. It's crucial that it is understood by all who read it (first-hand or forwarded on), so we achieve our objectives and cover everyone's needs.

Why include the word 'current' in the formula? This is because so often people systematically address the first two points I list, but then forget to update the information. Then the best-laid plans get messed up.

Here's an example. An external trainer is going to deliver a course for 10 members of a company's staff. One week earlier, their manager issues joining instructions to all attending. The course is to be held in the Byfield Room in a hotel the company uses. The trainer has been sent the full list of names and has asked the company to notify any changes before the day.

By the day of the training no changes have been communicated and the trainer arrives for set-up. He finds that the hotel has changed the venue to the Smithson Room, which has not been laid out as requested. There are no flipcharts and no projector screen.

By the time the course is due to start at 9 am, only seven attendees have turned up. The trainer calls the company to check but the relevant manager isn't available. So the trainer puts back the start time, in case the missing delegates are held up in traffic. He later finds out that the company knew that three delegates would be unable to attend on the day.

Can you see why the failure to relay changes cost money and affected performance? Both the hotel and the client company were at fault here. Although the course went ahead, there was unnecessary hassle and a distinct lack of professionalism. It also made for a chaotic scene which is likely to undermine delegates' perception of the day in total. This kind of thing happens all too frequently. It comes as a direct result of people not reading and responding, and messaging to update and inform others of changing or changed circumstances. A minor series of events can turn a well-organized programme into an unprofessional shambles.

# The Word Power Skills system: four easy steps to success

The system I now introduce appears in each book in the Better Business English series.

## *A guide to premier business writing*

The system uses the idea of 'a ladder of success', in which you start at the bottom (Step 1) and systematically climb to success (beyond Step 4) as follows:

## Step 1

Be correct:

- Know what your writing needs to achieve, alongside what your company needs to achieve.
- Reflect your company's values and personality and project 'brand you'.
- At the very least, match readers' minimum expectations.
- Ensure that your writing is free of mistakes.

Your business communication will fail if you get your basics wrong.

## Step 2

Be clear:

- Use plain English and express facts as simply as possible.
- Edit so that your main points are easily understood.
- Use headings and sub-headings to highlight key information.

Confused messages undermine your objectives. They can lose you custom too.

## Step 3

Make the right impact:

- Use the right words to grab attention and a layout that gets noticed for the right reasons.
- Paint a picture with your words and use verbs to convey action and ownership of who does what and when.
- Use the right style to present yourself and your company well.
- Create opportunities.

The right impact differentiates you from competitors and helps bring about the responses you need. There's lots of helpful detail about this in Chapter 4 on Social Media.

## Step 4

Focus on readers as your customers:

- Get to know about them as much as you can, so you can write from their perspective.
- Empathize with them and make your content interesting, so that they want to read.
- Favour positive, proactive words to engage, persuade, influence – and create a dialogue and following, where needed.
- Avoid words that put up barriers, and avoid unnecessary jargon.
- Instead choose words that convey a virtual handshake, to pull people towards you.

Use your written words to satisfy and, if possible, delight your customers.

# Your checklist for action

- Be aware that your readers and customers are likely to have a negative impression of (or reject) ineffective writing.
- Evaluate feedback on your writing. You can do this simply by checking your answers to questions such as the following:
  - When you send an e-mail, do people often not bother to read it?

- Do you have to send out the same message more than once to get the reply you need?
- Do people ever congratulate you or complain about the tone of your message?
- Are your letters, reports or e-mails significantly longer than those of your colleagues?
- When you receive new details, do you always update people who need to know?

- Understand the differences between academic English writing and business English writing.

- Remember business writing is results focused and tending to become more informal, especially because of the rise in e-writing where material is presented in bite-sized chunks.

- Be prepared to unlearn some of the rules you may have learnt at school – or now learn some you weren't taught!

# Chapter Three
# Quality matters

## Shine through your writing!

How do you want to be seen? What do you want to be remembered for? To be professional, it's best to get your business English writing right, first time and every time. Contribute to your own success by understanding that each bit of business writing you send out can be (indeed, should be) viewed as an advertisement for 'brand you' as well as for your company. Written words are 'frozen' in the point of time in which they were written: judged for what they are, when we're not there to explain them.

To succeed they have to be the right words for your commercial purpose, or you'll fall at the first hurdle. They also have to be right from your readers' point of view, or you'll fall at the second hurdle. And what a missed opportunity if you don't write to impress: to be the best you can. Don't settle for less: the competition won't!

## To make mistakes is only human?

The trouble is that whatever our proficiency in a language, we're all likely to make written mistakes sometimes. A tip that really works is: don't *expect* your writing to be right! You often achieve better results by expecting it to be wrong. That way you are more likely to:

- spot mistakes at draft stage;
- remove them before sending writing out;
- present a totally professional corporate image.

Checking, and even double-checking your writing before you send it can pay great dividends. You may spend longer than you would like at the planning stage but it raises the odds that each message you send out is right.

# How readers can react to written mistakes

Just take a look at three problematic sentences and let's see how readers might react.

> 1. Thank you for your order. You are demanded to send payment within 30 days.

First of all, the expression 'you are demanded' is not correct English. It's better to write something on the lines of 'Please send payment within 30 days' or 'You are requested to pay within 30 days.' In English there is an expression 'to demand payment' but it has a very strong connotation. It's generally used for the final notice before a company pursues legal action, to collect money owing to it in an overdue account. When the expression is used validly, it would be on the following lines:

> This is a final demand for payment (within 30 days) of your outstanding account.

So in our first example we have an outright grammatical mistake. But the wrong tone can also count as a writing mistake.

Let's look at the text again: 'Thank you for your order. You are demanded to send payment within 30 days.' Although the reader sees the initial words 'Thank you', the next sentence introduces a harsh, accusatory tone. Yet this is clearly one of the first points of contact between customer and company. The order has just been placed: 'Thank you for your order' tells us that. So is the customer going to feel that this is a nice company to do business with? I don't think so.

In business, we should ensure that when new customers place their orders, we make this a very positive experience for them. If a company can't be bothered to write well here, then the indicators are not good for future business success. Customers usually have a choice: there is likely to be an alternative company that they like to do business with. Which would you choose?

2. We can certainly provide the services you request in principal.

Homonyms are words that have the same or similar sound and sometimes the same spelling as another but whose meanings are different (more on this in Chapter 10). But let's just take a look here at two words that are frequently confused by native English and non-native English writers alike. They are:

Principal: an adjective generally meaning first in importance; also a noun meaning a chief or senior person, or an original sum of money for investment.

Principle: a noun meaning a fundamental truth or quality; a rule or belief governing a person's morally correct behaviour and attitudes.

In the second example, unfortunately the writer has chosen the wrong version of the homonym. The correct word would be 'principle'. Some readers may not mind this; some will not notice. But some will make a value judgement: this is wrong!

It may be unfair but just one wrong word can undermine readers' perception of a writer's or a company's professionalism. It can also distract readers' attention away from the writer's key message.

> 3. You should benefit us of further informations as we feel
> ourselves unable to help you.

This sentence contains some very common mistakes made by non-NE writers. 'You should benefit us' is not standard English. Nor is 'informations'. 'Information' exists only in the singular, no matter how much information is given (and incidentally, the same applies to 'training', though I often see 'trainings'). The second verb phrase, 'we feel ourselves', uses the reflexive form that English uses far less frequently than many other languages. When English uses it, it tends to be in a very physical, literal sense. Here it would mean 'we are actually touching ourselves'. It doesn't imply the state of mind that the writer assumes it means – and the sentence simply doesn't sound right. In Chapter 5 I will go into more detail on categories of English writers and speakers. This will further show you how, when it comes to business English, 'one size won't fit all'.

So, how might readers react to these mistakes? Well, on the first level, grammatical mistakes don't impress. On a second level, the writer sounds unhelpful. Once again is this really a company that is nice – or indeed easy – to do business with? And the very powerful word 'benefit' in business should be directed at customers, not us. So the writer has potentially made a big mistake here from the reader's perspective. If we rewrite the sentence as: 'Please could you let us have some further information so that we can help you?' then this helps get the message back on track. It's simpler and it works.

Although I've just highlighted some mistakes, I'm not suggesting a 'red pen' approach. Some managers use a red pen to highlight an employee's written mistakes, in a clearly unsupportive way. This approach really can demotivate staff and is best avoided.

It's true that sometimes you just have to write the way your line managers suggest. But it's always better to know the reasons why they consider one way better than another. Even in UK English you can opt to write certain words in two ways, both of which are correct. You can write 'recognize' or 'recognise', or 'judgement' or 'judgment' – and it can be personal or company preference that dictates which you use. If you don't understand the reasons why you must write a certain way, your manager owes it to you to explain why. But you also owe it to yourself to ask why.

It's in your own interests to know if you make mistakes. Readers may comment on them. In business you can't afford to 'bury your head in the sand' – in other words, just because you don't acknowledge something, that does not mean it does not exist! Problems do occur and every business needs to identify them. How else can we seek solutions and get things right?

Making mistakes may be human, but routinely making mistakes will never make good commercial sense. We do need to focus on quality, and it is a good idea to define what we mean by this. Does it mean top quality or simply acceptable? It's really up to each business to define what they expect the quality of their output to be – not just from their point of view but from customers' perspective. This lines up with one aspect of Step 1 on the ladder of success, described in Chapter 2.

# Further costs of getting your writing wrong

We saw how things can go wrong when we don't update written messages in the light of changed circumstances. The following scenario also shows the cost businesses can pay for getting writing wrong.

I submitted a database entry on my business to a company that was to include it in a Europe-wide guide. Their fee seemed reasonable, given the likely exposure to new business. I had to follow a restricted format and limited word count, so my entry was as follows:

---

### TQI Word Power Skills Training

Activity: A UK company that provides business support services for every type of business. It provides business English services to help with marketing literature and communication skills training.

Services include editing, text correction or fine tuning, quality assurance, proof-reading, group workshops, individual coaching in business English and cross-cultural briefing.

These innovative, fully confidential business services are designed to help you assure the quality of your service or product and help you hit your commercial target first and every time.

TQI Word Power Skills training offers businesses of all types and sizes expert and affordable solutions for their business English needs, together with international experience from previous consultancy in the Netherlands.

Co-operation request: TQI Word Power Skills Training seeks companies requiring these services.

---

A few weeks later I received an invoice from the company in charge of the database. Attached to this was a copy of the entry as it had actually appeared. Unknown to me, the copy had already gone live, Europe-wide, one month before I received the invoice. The entry was now the one shown below. It includes a number of errors, made when the company inputted my original wording onto the database. Can you spot these mistakes?

Quite understandably, I was not at all happy, especially when presented with an invoice to pay for this appalling entry. Can you see why this would be? If you look closely, you'll see there is at least one mistake in each paragraph. Some are spelling mistakes, such as 'infividual' for 'individual, 'breifing' for 'briefing'

### TQI Word Power Skills training

Activity: UK company that provides business support services for every type of business, it provides Business english services to help with marketing literature and communication skills training.

Services include editing, text correction or fine tuning, quality assurance, proof reading, group workshops, infividual coaching in Business English and inter cultural breifing.

These Innovative fully confidential business services are designed to help you assure the quality of your service or product and help you hit your commercial target first and every time.

TQI Word Power Skills training offers businesses of all types and sizes expert and affordable solutions for their business English needs, international expereince from previous consultancy in the Netherland.

Co-operation request: TQI Word Power Skills Training seeks companies that require there servces.

and 'expereince' for 'experience'. Some are inconsistencies, such as business English and Business English. Both may be used, but it's better style to keep to a single use, certainly within one paragraph. The word innovative suddenly has a capital 'I', thus we find 'Innovative' even though the word is mid-sentence. And so on – the list goes on. One thing is sure: nobody ran a spellcheck or grammar check.

What ultimately was the cost of this regrettable incident? The answer is that there was a cost to pay on a number of different levels. I refused to pay the invoice because the entry was incorrect, so the company suffered the loss of that income. That company then had to redraft a correct entry, and replace the incorrect entry at their own cost. The cost to my company was in terms of undermined professional credibility (both in the short and long term).

You can easily see how such an apparently low-key set of mistakes can have a disastrous effect on the professional credibility of a company that's operating internationally.

In the final analysis, although the mistakes were not mine, they appeared to be mine. It was my company name and my details that appeared... which leads me to the next section.

# You can never fully outsource your writing

What that last episode taught me was this: not to assume that because the version I sent for publishing was correct, the published version would be correct too. The advertising company used Apple Macs and did not just cut and paste my Word document: they retyped the copy themselves. Whether or not this was the case, I should have asked to see the final proof before publication. Printers often provide this as a matter of course, to cover themselves against complaints at a later stage. But note that word 'often'... it is not the same as 'always'!

If you outsource something and it goes wrong, the backlash becomes yours. You cannot outsource responsibility!

# Checking for mistakes

Let me reinforce the message: expect mistakes in your writing draft. Here's an analogy. When I was learning to drive, my teacher gave me invaluable advice. I was told to imagine everyone on the road was a maniac. That way, he explained, I would always be alert to the fact that mistakes inevitably happen. What's more, I would be a better driver as a result. Far from being complacent, I would be more likely to respond quickly to ever-changing situations and take corrective action. Can you see how easily the advice applies to checking for mistakes in your English writing too?

# Proofreading tips

Check everything you write before you send it out. Here are tips to help:

- Allow sufficient time for your proofreading. If you rush, you may still overlook the mistakes you are looking for.

- It can be easier to proofread on paper than on a computer screen (though be eco-friendly about this).

- Use a standard or online dictionary or grammar book to help you, or your computer's spelling and grammar check (set on the correct variant of English for your target audience). Do be aware that this is not fail-safe. It may let the wrong word(s) through, especially homonyms, for example 'brake' for 'break', 'there' for 'their' and so on.

- Watch out for auto-correct wrongly changing your correct words such as 'its' to 'it's' or 'definitely' to 'defiantly'.

- Try reading your lines backwards (people sometimes use a ruler to read one line at a time, to avoid distraction). You do not check for meaning this way, you just check that the words are written correctly.

- Check for meaning and logical arrangement.

- Make a self-help list of any words that you regularly get wrong, so that you can check them quickly and effectively next time you write them.

# Your checklist for action

- Understand that mistakes can and do happen.
- Make sure that you take steps to minimize this, such as running spellcheck and grammar check in the right variety of English.

- Understand that mistakes in your English are not just about spelling and grammar.

- They can also be when words are left out, when sentences confuse or present facts in a disorderly way that distorts the correct message.

- Understand the longer-term impact mistakes may have (and how these can in turn impact on you and your company).

- Highlight to others the importance of correct English writing.

- Always check your writing before you issue it.

- If you are not sure, ask for help from someone who will know.

# Chapter Four
# Telling your story through social media

## There's a new type of business writing

Just as the printing press revolutionized the way written communication could spread messages far and wide, so a new type of communication has turned the business world inside out. It's all about harnessing the power of social media, which I'll explain in detail in this chapter.

Step back just a few years... and who could have believed the impact social media has had, and will continue to have, on the way we write? The 'new kid on the block' is increasingly edging out other forms of written messages. Rather than social media's style being affected by traditional writing, it's the other way round, as I'll show. Companies that side-line its importance have a lot to lose. The winners are those who acknowledge the importance of this new, ambitious front-runner.

Social media requires an integrated approach – and we need to adopt a distinctly conversational style in our writing. For some the style comes naturally; for more traditional writers it can seem rather daunting. So in this chapter, there will be some line-by-line analysis, but we'll also immerse ourselves in the fuller picture to see how the social media 'storyline' fits together.

# Get into the social media mindset

From the simple sharing of a message to in-depth conversation, to following the latest news, to opening transactions and closing deals, social media is an intrinsic part of our modern world. Incidentally, I'm describing 'social media' as a collective singular here, in the sense of the activity on social media. Grammatically, it would also be correct to write that social media 'are' part of our world.

If you can write, not only are you improving your career prospects generally, you can also deal with any social media, where the written word takes centre stage. What you need to write depends on your personal and company story, the points you want to make, the goals you need to achieve, and how you write to attract and maintain readers' interaction with you, as the story evolves.

This chapter is about getting you involved. You need a mindset that can put a winning combination together. It's very much about projecting 'brand personality' into this new form of conversational writing.

So, first I'll explain what social media is; then I will immerse you in some informative case studies on how successful companies write for it. We'll examine the techniques used, so you can choose which suit your organization. Then I'll provide tips on how to write for the various platforms.

# More about social media

Social media is all about sharing information and collaborating online, bringing the facility to enable everyone to get in touch with anyone, anywhere, anytime. In business, although the biggest players have the biggest budget, they can't get complacent.

Even the smallest voice now has a megaphone to communicate globally, be part of the conversation – and go viral.

Responsive companies of all sizes need to get serious about the fact that most online presence today is on social media – and written content is king, as even the very best visuals won't work by themselves.

People constantly check their networks and they want to be kept posted on things such as helpful information, breaking news, innovation, events, offers etc.

Increasingly, written content needs to be suitable for the fast-growing use of mobile devices, including the new wave of smart watches. Users are increasingly 'on the go', maybe waiting for a train or between meetings. They need easily highlighted messages and to know at a glance where you're leading. We're seeing the 'click here' that was right for the laptop, change to 'read more'.

We now see social media used alongside, sometimes in place of, traditional leaflets or mailing. Words even take centre stage in the fast-growing messaging via video or pictures with captions. Every message has been (or should have been) finely crafted by that business. Being social offers the opportunity (and expectation) to talk not just about brand, products and services but also to introduce personalities: the people behind the brand. There's more opportunity for storytelling that resonates and a huge demand for customized messages to elicit buy-in or positive reaction. The Word Power Skills system shown in Chapter 2 is immensely valuable, as the challenge (and the exciting part) is how to get your words heard through the noise. How to adapt, to keep up with the trends and even create them?

English has such an advantage, being used extensively across multiple platforms. But if English is not your company's first language or that of your social media writers, remember the points made earlier in the book. Words that are right for your home market may not work abroad, even where English is the common language.

As an example, let's look at this wording on sportswear brand Adidas' global website:

> Go get better, share your skills, compare yourself with the best and challenge your friends.

It uses very clear wording, easily understandable on first reading. Let's contrast this with wording used their Adidas India website:

> Criticism and self-doubt can paralyze the most talented athletes. Only a rare breed converts the stones thrown at them into milestones…

The language is rather more poetic and thought-provoking. It requires a more sophisticated understanding of the English used.

Coca-Cola is one of the most recognized global brands and it too adapts the English it uses across the world. So although we see the social media hashtag #PerfectCoke globally, some countries won't necessarily understand #SwelterStopper used for ice-cool Coke or #SarapNgFirst – 'the first time taste of the #PerfectCoke experience'. This latter example purposefully features Tagalog-English to resonate with their target youth market in the Philippines.

If you decide to outsource any of your social media (especially likely if you export), or if you simply collaborate with other partners, don't forget you are ultimately accountable for the messages you put out. This charity found this out to their cost, despite their best intentions:

## CASE STUDY Samaritans Charity

Samaritans are a highly respected UK charity, offering support to anyone in emotional distress.

Looking for ways of helping vulnerable people online (especially those aged 18–35), they hired a digital agency to help them launch the #SamaritansRadar app. This sent an alert to users when people they followed posted messages that algorithms picked up to suggest depressed or suicidal thoughts.

The app was withdrawn almost immediately after attracting criticism that it didn't work. It certainly failed on a semantic level, as one Twitter user showed. He added the #SamaritansRadar hashtag to his innocuous post: 'Making a mixtape of smooth jazz classics. Maybe I should end it all with a bit of Alfonzo Blackwell. #SamaritansRadar.'

The algorithm had mistakenly picked up on the words 'maybe I should end it all' as alluding to suicide.

# What are the key objectives?

These include: engage, be shared and convert – by being relevant, useful, knowledgeable, credible, consistently professional and personable. All your corporate communications need to reflect your values and your personality – and achieve your goals.

Your focus always has to be about creating good-quality content and connectivity between your website and your social media posts. How engaged both are, affects your visibility and could impact on your Search Engine Optimization (SEO) ranking. Google's guidelines for SEO state that pages must be written primarily for users, not for search engines: '#1: Focus on the user and all else will follow.' This rings true for social media generally.

Beyond that you will need:

- a clear structure that's easy to read;
- clear links;
- to engage social signals that are likely to improve your visibility.

Social signals (which Google and other search engines pick up) mean the interaction your website and social media posts are gaining (visits, likes, shares, dialogue etc). It's about realizing that you're no longer just broadcasting, you need to be part of the conversation – and a listener too. When everyone is an author, make sure you're part of the content that's valued. Write things of interest, offer deals, project a brand that engages, get involved – and show you're interested too.

Look at this Facebook offer from Pizza Express (fast-food company).

## CASE STUDY    Create your new favourite pizza

Pizza Express posted a Facebook offer, inviting diners to join them in celebrating their new Spring menu. Their enticement was: 'create your own pizza to feature on our Autumn menu.' The winning pizza would join the favourites on their menu and '£10,000 AND a holiday for two to the Amalfi Coast could all be yours!'

Emblazoned at the side of the page was: 'Free Dough Balls for every entry!' ie every entrant is actually a winner.

The success of the offer is in the result and they were instantly eliciting positive interaction, such as: 'Thanks/Cheers/BIG THANKS!!/A fairly amazing prize bundle, and a fun competition too! They've done a really nice job with that competition...'

Let's analyse the components of their successful writing:

1    There was a compelling headline that appealed to the individual reader.

2 There was a great offer – not just the chance of the 'fairly amazing prize bundle' as one reader put it, but also a freebie for every entrant.

3 For discoverability, the tags were 'holiday' and 'Pizza Express'.

4 There was also link to their website and Pizza Express Deals.

Look out for examples for yourself. See what you feel works, and you're sure to find writing that:

- expresses key messages in the right channel, in language that's right for the expectations, needs, aspirations and interests of the target audience on that platform (casual? more formal? culture? age-related? etc);
- has compelling headlines that attract target readers' attention (more on this shortly);
- communicates even complex messages simply (links can take readers to detail needed);
- maintains interest and credibility (readers must trust you to know links will take them to something professional/of value, otherwise why click?);
- is current (you can refresh useful content, as I'll show shortly).

Your business objectives are usually any or all of the following:

- to increase brand awareness and 'be part of the conversation' (as positively as possible);
- to get your messages across and, depending on your business, to boost sales;
- to create ongoing dialogue, listen to customers and improve;
- to gain market insights;

- to share valuable information, develop and maintain relationships;
- to get your messages found widely through SEO.

## Some major platforms out there

Businesses need to choose the channels that best suit their needs – and also those of their target demographic. You can't just expect everyone to open a Facebook or Twitter account in order to engage with you. Choose channels you know your audience is interested in too (and remember that not everyone wants to be on the same channel) and that you can invest time in. Then get social, otherwise how can you expect to create a loyal following or generate leads?

Douglas Ray, a multimedia producer at Three Ships Media, created an amusing, helpful 'donut' analogy, which people adapt regularly, and which describes the feel of some major platforms right now:

- Twitter – I'm eating a #donut.
- Facebook – I like donuts.
- YouTube – here I am eating my donut.
- Pinterest – here's a photo and recipe for donuts.
- Instagram – here's a vintage photo of my donut.

As more channels get added to the mix, including WhatsApp, Viber etc (forms of chat that sit between original text messaging and the more recent instant messaging – see Chapter 7) and Google+, recognize and adapt to their style. Keep your purpose in mind: be clear.

# How do companies shine through their social media interaction?

There's been a shift in focus from product or service (the focus of traditional writing) to consumer in social media. So your writing will need to be:

- always reader-focused and less about direct selling (this doesn't completely rule out selling, depending on what each channel allows in terms of promotion);
- more about your voice and your brand personality.

Share information and experiences of value, the newest this, the helpful that, etc. If people value your content, they can become 'brand advocates', without ever meeting you. You're likely to reciprocate and this can open new dialogues and horizons.

Learn by looking at how companies shine through their online interaction. This case study highlights how one company succeeds.

**CASE STUDY** Innocent Drinks

Innocent Drinks are a successful UK soft drinks company. They are known not just for their drinks but also for their 'quirky' offline and online brand presentation.

At the time of writing, they have an enviable 471,691 Facebook page likes – achieved, I think, through their positive and reactive customer interaction. They are not the biggest player in the sector but in their market, interest and responsiveness can be the differentiator.

If we look at their social media feeds, they often use the same content across channels. Keeping it innovative, current and something that they want people to share, they devised a #chainofgood Compliment Generator. They post this on their blog and Facebook page, introducing it with a strap line about their product: 'tastes good, does you good, does others good.' A short write-up follows on how their drinks have natural goodness, and how 10 per cent of profits go to charity.

Visitors to the #chainofgood are invited to choose and post a compliment from the 'Compliment Generator' such as 'You are a walking high-five' (10,000 Facebook shares, 4,282 Tweets). The element of choice means the words will be right for their readers' readers too. They also invite suggestions, to enhance appeal and interaction. The overall effect is to spread positive brand awareness.

Keeping current and relevant, the company adapts the generator for occasions such as downloadable cards for Mother's Day, complete with company logo.

The style in the following tweet is a million miles away from the Innocent approach. It's sent by a 'social media' company as their standard 'first point of contact' tweet, to all people they have started following on Twitter:

@ (name of person they follow) Do you blog?

Would it surprise you that no one appears to reply? It's abrupt (which is different to being concise) and doesn't show any interest in the person they question. One gets the feeling that the company tweets only so they can sell their blogging services.

# Writing that creates trust can create a community

Building a community through social media is not just for commercial brands. We now find many more social enterprises setting up, not just in traditional third sector activity areas such as health and social care, education and community services, but also in traditional private sector activities. Most encouragingly, we see companies who want to use their profits for the public good.

Charismatic retail magnate Theo Paphitis is one such supporter of skills and entrepreneurship. The following case study shows how he created a supportive small business community via social media.

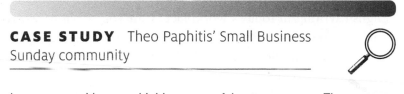

**CASE STUDY** Theo Paphitis' Small Business Sunday community

In common with many highly successful entrepreneurs, Theo Paphitis is open about his dyslexia, which has actually afforded him an advantage in understanding the importance of simple, vibrant, well-chosen words to sell messages, products and services and create a following.

He realized how helpful it would be to small businesses in the UK (known to be the lifeblood of the economy), to understand that writing with impact on social media – via professional, mobile-friendly devices and websites – was a powerful tool for networking and growth.

To this end, he created Small Business Sunday (shortened to the hashtag #SBS on Twitter). Each week, he rewards small businesses that tweet him @TheoPaphitis and write about their businesses in one tweet (with hashtag #SBS) in a dedicated time slot, on a Sunday. He then retweets his favourite lucky six, judged on how well they have communicated their message. As he has over 450,000 followers, this provides them with a massive publicity boost.

Theo continues to build this #SBS community not only with offers and by staging events for winners, but also by providing a website for interaction within the community itself. He and his group of companies actively get involved in the conversation.

In his words:

My vision is that everyone who has ever won an #SBS re-tweet
from me becomes part of a friendly club. Like-minded individuals
can share successes and learnings... I know I have been lucky in
business and I am keen now to spread goodwill to others, of course
not forgetting that very often you make your own luck by making use
of every opportunity.

This and similar cases are very exciting applications of business
English writing in today's workplace. Can you see how, where
English is a common language, such skilful use of social media
to build communities can be rolled out – not simply on a local
basis but nationally and internationally too?

# The long and the short of it: past, present and future

It's not just short posts that can go viral. Now 'everyone is a
writer' – but not everyone is willing or able to write good material in depth. Articles with detailed information can be highly
valuable.

Digital Storytelling has become a big focus of online marketing and aims at encouraging user-generated content (UGC).
Naturally you must write the right information so people find
your posts. Without discoverability, you won't get shared! So
provide the right links, photos, etc.

Your stories can be brief but sometimes it's the detail that
makes them come alive. That's the beauty of being able to provide a link in your short post to a fuller article on your website
or elsewhere.

As part of the story, consider intriguing your readers – maybe hold some information back, so they want to explore further. A link can take them to that valuable 'more'. But avoid 'clickbait' – the pejorative term to describe captivating links that only take you to spam advertisements etc.

## CASE STUDY  Ogilvy and Mather

Ogilvy and Mather, the most awarded advertising agency in the world, intersperse old and new content, and long and short blogs/articles, to create and retain interest.

They embrace the iconic status of their founder, original 'Mad Man' David Ogilvy. His words of 1982 still ring true: 'People who think well, write well. Woolly minded people write woolly memos, woolly letters and woolly speeches.'

The agency regularly posts his quotes on their website, Facebook page and Twitter feed. They routinely mix and match language of the past with today's, as this Facebook 'Ogilvyism' post (with 1,500 views) shows:

> Disruption of convention. Disruption of rules. Disruption of received wisdom. Disruption of 'we've always done it this way'. #ThoughtLeadership #Inspire

They then provide a link to a much fuller and perennially valuable 'years-old article' by David Ogilvy, on the importance of stimulating creativity and innovation, through information and reflection.

The important thing is that all your posts work towards a common goal. Are you going to post similar material across the platforms you use? Whatever you do, the messages need to harmonize.

> **Activity:** It's not just the big players who can seize an opportunity to link new posts to the history of success their company has built. Can you rejig a good past post of yours, to make it relevant today? Are there tips you can share, even re-share? The principles of great communication work across channels, even across ages.

# Further writing tips for key channels such as Facebook, Twitter, LinkedIn

## *Facebook*

Facebook is currently the world's largest social networking site and so offers enormous potential for going viral. You may consider this a strong case for using global rather than local English (see Chapter 5).

When writing a company Facebook page, create relationships with users. Show you are there to do business with them. Be interesting; offer something to attract visitors to your page and get them to hit the 'Like' button: a visible approval of a product or service.

Writing tips to help are:

- Be authentic, let readers see your personality, on a professional basis.

- Keep personal comments for your personal accounts, have a corporate policy for Facebook posts.

- Ask fans/'likers' for feedback on your product/services via questions in posts, or links to surveys.

- Post good news on your business: sector-specific general updates; insightful, people-based anecdotes about your organization; only use humour that will work for your audience/culture.

- Share YouTube video clips and other visuals of general interest, as well as about your business.

- Reply to comments. Thank people for positive comments and post promptly with your viewpoint, to counter any negative comments.

I'm sure many of you will have passed a positive message about a company on to others and, in a sense, become an unpaid advocate of their brand. Take a look at the language they used that engaged your interest. It's a fascinating exercise that can help your writing.

## *Twitter*

Twitter is a real-time information network where you simply find the accounts you find most compelling and follow the conversations.

Each short burst of information is called a Tweet. Limited to 140 characters, it's essential to express key points concisely. Photos, video and other links can add to the story.

Tips for businesses writing on Twitter include the tips I've given for Facebook, as well as:

- Algorithms prove that content that's helpful gets found and shared. This can be tips on things that work or problems to avoid, inspirational quotes, universal truths, or something relating to a trending topic etc.

- You can actively ask people to share your information: 'please share' or 'please retweet' can work if your content is good.

- Analyse which tweets are getting retweeted or 'favorited'.

- Post your tweets in the right time zone for your potential global readers. Twitter is fast-moving and transient, so re-post tweaked tweets at differing intervals – and double-check for mistakes before you post. Speed can trap you into making them!

- Hashtags are useful for introducing topics of general interest and are searchable, for example #BusinessCommunication or #globalprojects.

- The name you write under (your 'Twitter handle') and your Twitter bio can provide an opportunity to describe what you do and/or your brand (mine is @wordpowerskills – do say hello!)

Where writers err is when the message is all about *them* and nothing to do with others. What do you think of this tweet sent to me as a direct message (DM)?

Hey what do you do? I deliver strategic digital transformation. Come over and like my Facebook page!

If you have written a good bio, complete with your website details, any tweet writer (tweep, tweeter etc) should have the courtesy to read the outline of what you do, before making contact in this way. This tweet is actually about them. And would you talk this person directly, without introduction or further evidence, in any other business situation? Also you can't assume that a Twitter user will be on Facebook.

As social media is about writing for people – not robots – in accessible, conversational language, I think tweet 2 below generally works better for the medium than tweet 1:

1 There's little doubt about it, it feels rather good that my business writing book appears to be useful as it's selling.

2 Woohoo, so pleased: my book is in the #businesswriting charts because it helps! Thank you so much! #lovemyreaders

But if the style is too effusive for your target audience, don't use it. Use your judgement – and, as I mention throughout, it's a must to have a policy on language that's off limits, eg expletives/religious/political/sexist/racist comments.

Remember also that people use Twitter to make immediate complaints. If your company is involved, be sure to monitor for them and deal with them quickly. Others will be watching how you deal with this too.

## Newsletters, blogs, vlogs or micro-blog posts

Newsletters and blogs read like articles and inform. Whilst printed newsletters and other material have to explain background within the articles themselves, online newsletters, blogs, vlogs (video logs) or micro-blogs (such as Twitter posts) can easily refer to detailed information elsewhere online. Post regularly to keep material fresh and build up a readership that you hope will be loyal advocates.

Keep your paragraphs shorter than in print (some recommend four sentences maximum). As reading on a computer screen can be tiring, and reading on mobile devices can be 'on the go', you need to 'grab eyeballs' so people do read. Invite questions and comments (and reply buttons) – as long as you plan to respond to these. Get involved with others' blogs too. Be discoverable and maintain visibility.

**CASE STUDY** Sir Richard Branson and the Virgin Group

Sir Richard Branson, the highly successful founder of the Virgin Group, is known for his inspirational blogs. He gives valuable advice in one of his posts as a LinkedIn Influencer, on how he manages to write and avoid writer's block:

What do you talk to your friends about? What was that interesting article you read the other day? What was everyone chatting about in the office at lunch? Could there be a blog in that? More than likely, yes.

He advises keeping it personal, as inauthenticity is easy to sniff out. If it wasn't really him writing on LinkedIn or posting his virgin.com blogs, people would spot it a mile off. He loves sharing what's happening in his world and the latest happenings at Virgin, and can think of no better way of doing it than in real time, online.

If we analyse his blogs, they are often very short. One blog in 2015 simply read:

'The difference is in the difference'. That sums up his philosophy that if you aren't making and expressing a difference then you shouldn't be in business.

He then asks for readers' comments on the business difference they are trying to achieve. His words 'I'd love to hear about it' show his interest and encourage interaction: the hallmark of successful social media writing.

This short blog (tags: inspiration, business, quotes) achieved 11,100 shares, with a breakdown: 687 Facebook likes, 3,186 Tweets, 2,100 Google+ and 5,100 LinkedIn shares. There are also links to: 'My Top 10 Quotes on Leadership' and 'My Top 10 Quotes on Failure'.

So if we analyse his writing:

1  he often uses an intriguing headline;

2  he writes simple, universal truths expressed in his easy, conversational style, reinforced by personal brand;

3  his business messages reach out to an inclusive 'you';

4  there's a call to action in an engaged style.

We see this mix of easy language elsewhere on Virgin websites, for example in their Help forums – 'Settle in and get comfy, we'd love to see you get involved' – as part of how customers experience the brand.

Virgin definitely do not ignore the business of selling. In all posts, we still see traditional calls to action such as 'Sign up to our newsletter', 'Hurry!', 'Online exclusive offer' or 'Don't miss out'.

It's not surprising people love sharing this advice, as it takes the fear away from the task. People feel a lot less nervous when they adopt this approach.

## LinkedIn and SlideShare

LinkedIn is a networking site for matters strictly related to business and careers etc. Blatant selling of products or services is disallowed. But employers do trawl for new talent on it, so write a great profile, showcasing your attributes (whether as a provider or seeker), so it can double up as a résumé/CV. Avoid words that LinkedIn identify as clichés (more on this in Chapter 11).

Use LinkedIn's dynamic extra features to help you project 'brand you' and make yourself discoverable. Start with a headline that sums up who you are and what you want

Here are some fictitious examples:

1 Bart Wierks – Improving IT Systems * Seeking Career Opportunity.

2 Carl Chapman – Change Management Guru 'Hire me and results guaranteed'.

3 Monica Heiss – Senior Associate at XYZ Global Staffing Associates * 4,000 connections

In example 1, we see at a glance what Bart does and what he's seeking. In example 2, Carl uses rather more expressive language. His words express his personal brand and self-belief. In example 3, Monica feels that her position and her networking credentials speak for themselves. Which style, if any, do you think works best? How would you write?

Do also consider posting your own interesting content on SlideShare, a LinkedIn company that's the world's largest professional content sharing platform. It's a great way of getting noticed professionally.

# What excites people so much they want to share it?

You already have an idea about this and indeed, analysing across all channels, these messages get shared most:

- Lists and tips – especially things on how to work better, for example, 'How Successful People Stay Calm'; 'The Three Qualities of People I Most Enjoy Working With'; 'Ten Top Tips for Leadership'.

- Articles that bring out an emotional response – positive emotions get faster response on most channels, eg greatest, happiest, cutest, wow this is GREAT! That doesn't mean that negative emotions don't work, however. 'Four Destructive Myths to Banish' definitely gets shared. 'Do you know how many things you could be sued for?' will most likely work better for an insurer than 'We introduce our exciting new insurance product!' But choose your negatives carefully in a business context.

- Quotes – as with articles, people share emotions just as much (maybe more) than they share facts. Share others' words of wisdom or witticisms etc, and you can become part of the chatter. If the quotes are your own, you may have more influence – and lead the conversation.

- Verbs – whether knowledge or action-based, for example: know, prove, think, grab one now, hurry, don't miss out. (There is more on this in Chapter 10.)

- Captivating captions/slogans that underpin and enhance a relevant and brilliant visual/picture/video – for example, Apple: *Think different*. Nike: *Just do it*. KitKat: *Have a break… have a Kit Kat*. (Just listen to the sound of the 'k' in the Kit Kat slogan. You can almost hear the sound of the biscuit breaking! That's effective writing.)

Alliteration can also help engagement – for brands such as PayPal, Coca-Cola, Dunkin' Donuts as well as for articles or videos: 'Colloquialisms Can Confuse'.

- Posts with calls to action (more on this shortly).
- Facts and infographics.

See how Step 3 in the Word Power Skills system in Chapter 2 – 'Make the right impact' – will help you greatly here.

When online, you might like to check how global media company Buzzfeed Inc. master digital sharing of 'the most social content on the web'. Notice how they customize the home page for the country, eg United States, Australia, India etc. Get a feel for what might work for you. But don't lift copy or images and use them as your own or you could face plagiarism charges.

# Call people to action – and check it's worked

An important element of social media is checking that it worked. If you go unnoticed, it might as well be money down the drain. So it never harms to hammer home this message: build in effective calls to action as if your life depended on it. You want people to react. Better, you want them to discuss positively, even evangelize. Mostly in business we need buy-in and sales. Ogilvy and Mather aren't afraid to state: 'We sell or else'.

Express, where feasible, what you want people to do next, *in all your written tasks*. Your focus in social media may be selling messages about brand, but you can still hope to convert to sales at a later date. Invite readers to subscribe to your newsletter or contact you. You can ask people:

- to *share* some piece of content (industry insights, other knowledge, observations, news, your own tips etc) or your brand;

- to *like* on Facebook; or
- to *retweet* what you say (evangelism can achieve sales too).

The hard fact is that without sales and profits, your core business can flounder.

## Tips for writing calls to action

- Explain *why* (one or more major benefits) and *how* people should respond.
- Communicate clearly what customers will get.
- Offer a realistic deadline and the benefits for the customer by acting quickly (a free offer/discount/upgrade/limited edition/pegged interest rates etc).
- Highlight dates or events that can be useful to your demographic. The more national, multicultural or international you become or want to become, the more hooks you can use, eg Christmas, Sinterklaas, Thanksgiving, Diwali etc.
- By showing you understand issues of relevance to the world out there (where your current and prospective clients reside) you can become the trusted friend that they will turn to for advice. Once they see that your advice comes from a place of values and knowledge, they are more likely to pay for targeted advice from 'that trusted friend' – or at least be an advocate for you to others.

Don't 'overthink' when you write. Don't lose sight of the essence of your business that needs to be written throughout your business, from your business cards on!

## Your social media posts need to cross-refer to your website

Writing for websites isn't within the scope of this chapter or indeed this book. It's important to mention, though, that it does need to act as a hub for your social media posts. All content should cross-refer and have a consistent look, feel and corporate style as part of the reader experience. So, just as with your social media posts, do your messages stand out with the 'power words' that reflect your values? Was your website originally written in a traditional style? Might you now have to rewrite, to align with how you write for social media – and to suit mobile devices?

Now people expect bite-sized messages, headlined and subheadlined to break up text for scan reading. More than ever now, captions have a role to play in explaining the visuals you use. Make them discoverable.

Finally, if your website is in English, do you use this in a global or local context? With the potential to reach out to new territories via social media too, writing effectively in English means one size won't fit all.

## Telling your story

We've looked at many examples of how companies project their voice and personality in social media and how they tell their brand story, drawing readers into it and being interested in readers' stories too.

By now you should have a definite idea of what story you have to tell, alongside your company's personality. It's your exciting challenge to write vibrant content that draws people towards you.

So what's your compelling story? What did it begin with? Where are you at? Where are you going? Are you going to let readers share your people's stories and see their personalities? And are you going to invite your audience to share their stories?

There are no rights and wrongs here. This approach may not work for all but it allows you to understand principles behind the mindset required in writing for social media. As a checklist we could add:

- Never lose sight of your objectives and your readers' needs and expectations.
- How will you adapt your tone for the demographic you target?
- How will you get them to respond?
- How will you maintain interaction, as positively as possible?
- Are you asking the right questions? Are you getting the answers you hope for?
- Who will be there to respond to their questions – or their complaints, if any? (In social media, people expect rapid response.)
- How could your communication better lead to building the community you desire?

This chapter has shown you how companies write for these social media platforms for different reasons. They are largely to do with a desire to get individuals to help them get their name out there, even go viral, to develop and maintain a good global reputation. Just as a company needs to be responsive to customers when writing for social media, it needs to respond by revising corporate writing generally, as times move on. Just as business writing expressions such as 'hereunder', 'the afore-said', 'we remain your obedient servants' and so on have been ditched over the past few decades, companies need to identify what becomes currently mainstream. Language evolves so policies need to as well, otherwise widely differing corporate styles can confuse readers and work against brand.

Everything has to be consummately professional because reputation matters – and it's easy for inferior writing to go viral for all the wrong reasons!

# Your checklist for action

- How do you plan to write for social media? What are your objectives? Which channels will you use?

- How are you going to communicate your personality, as well as your values?

- Design writing that is discoverable by and relevant to your target audience.

- Be social when you write; get involved and maintain interaction, so that you create a following/community and benefit from loyal brand advocates.

- Don't see social media writing as an inferior form of business communication; be professional and mind your and others' reputation. Mistakes can rapidly go viral.

- Check that everyone in your company, as well as in any outside agency you hire, understands how to project your voice: sometimes personal, always corporate.

- Keep up with emerging channels; tailor your writing and formatting for readers' business and cultural expectations.

- Analyse the language used in posts that work (these can be others' posts, not just your own); adapt your vocabulary and understand that language evolves.

- Ensure that your message is consistent across all your communication channels.

- Use the Word Power Skills writing system as it will continue to work across emerging channels too.

# Chapter Five
# Defining business English

Y ou may at first glance think that this chapter is not for you. Some of the definitions I'm going to outline come more from the world of education. But it really will help you if you work in a multicultural team, a cosmopolitan office, a multinational organization, or have a potential global reach through social media. The moment we realize the challenges those around us may also face with workplace writing is the moment we learn how to write better ourselves.

So let's get a bit more specific here if you want to find out more. We know English is a major language of commercial communication and a world language of the internet and of global access to knowledge. Business English is the name given to the English used for dealing with business communication in English – though you will find many variants, as I'll shortly explain. This can present unexpected problems unless you understand how to design your communication to give you the best chance of success for your target audience.

## 'Standard' and 'variant' English

A particularly interesting fact is that globally there are more non-native speakers of English than native English speakers. Projections indicate that by 2020, 2 billion people worldwide will be learning or teaching English. So English is certainly no longer the preserve of the nation that gives the language its name. It belongs to no single culture; instead it is something that acts as a bridge across borders and cultures.

Years ago when I first worked abroad, I saw the commercial need to help multinationals seize the competitive edge in their use of English as a global business language. It was then that I realized how puzzled both foreigners and native English speakers can be by the way English is used. Often it's because non-native English speakers use it in unconventional ways. It is also often because people don't realize that UK or British English is not exactly the same as the many other variations of business English that exist. These include US or American English, Australian English, Caribbean English, Indian English, Singapore English and South African English. You can see how extensive the list is.

Business communication is crucial to success. So if people are puzzled by that communication, this is bad news. Getting the right messages out and receiving the right answers are the life-blood of commercial success. I found it helped my clients communicate effectively cross-culturally when I showed them how to follow some norms of commonly accepted 'standard' English. The result? People understood each other! Internal as well as external customers were better able to buy in to things put to them.

So what is 'standard' English? I use the expression to mean the English routinely described in mainstream English dictionaries and grammar books. It's the English used throughout this book, likely to be understood by all users.

Unless I indicate otherwise, the spelling and grammar used are the UK English variety requested by my publishers, to follow their house style. One of the challenges in writing UK English is that there can be more than one correct way of spelling certain words, as I've mentioned earlier. For example: recognize and recognize, judgment and judgement, e-mail and email can all be used correctly in UK English. Some people give explanations for these differences that are too simplistic, saying that 'recognize' indicates an American English spelling. But this is only part of the picture – and you will find more on variant spellings later in the book.

So there are times when I may refer to US English as well, where there are clearly divergent spellings or meanings. But the book won't address spelling and grammatical differences between UK and US English in detail. The important thing is: know that you need to check.

This takes me to my next point. Whenever we write and whatever we write, we must understand the conventions to follow, if we are to please our target readers. If necessary, explain at the outset the convention you are following, so you can avoid unfounded or unnecessary criticism. One thing is sure: if someone can find grounds for criticizing writing, they will! So be one step ahead and, if you are asked, be able to name not only which variant you are using but also why.

Be consistent, because consistency in approach underpins a strong, quality-conscious corporate image. You undermine this if some people in your company use UK English spellcheck and grammar check and others use US English versions in their standard corporate communication. It happens all the time, often without people realizing.

Just as this book is not about 'taking you back to school', it's not even necessarily about gaining the proficiency of a native English speaker. I have already hinted that not all native speakers are proficient! Instead, the book is all about reaching the level of competence you need in order to succeed in everything you write.

# Writing for both native and non-native English speakers

For ease of reference, you'll already have noticed that when I refer to native English speakers this means anyone who speaks any variety of English as their first language.

If you are a non-native English speaker, you may know these categories: English as an acquired language (EAL), English as a foreign language (EFL), English for speakers of other languages (ESOL) – all of which are self-explanatory – and English as a second language (ESL). The book is suitable for all and terms I use are:

- *native English (NE) speaker or writer* to mean someone whose first language is English, and native English (NE) writing to refer to their writing;

- *non-native English (non-NE) speaker or writer* to mean someone whose first language is not English, and non-native English (non-NE) writing to refer to their writing.

# Some surprising problems with English for global business

The fact that English is used so extensively for global business yields quite a surprising result. It means that written business English is ultimately directed more at a non-native English audience than at a native English audience. As well as there being different varieties of English, there are, in effect, sub-varieties directly caused by mixing English with the language patterns of the native country. Examples are Chinglish (Chinese-English), Manglish (Malaysian-English) and Singlish (Singapore-English). The same phenomenon can happen in any language mix.

Sometimes this can lead to out-and-out mistranslations. Although users may understand what they mean, these can be unintentionally funny or unintelligible to the foreign reader, as the following real-life mistranslated signs show. I deliberately don't highlight the countries concerned as it would be unfair to single any out. These mistakes occur across the board!

- Sign over an information booth: Question Authority
- Sign in maternity ward: No children allowed

- Sign in restaurant: Customers who find our waitresses rude ought to see our manager
- In an airline ticket office: We take your bags and send them in all directions
- In a hotel lift/elevator: Please leave your values at the front desk

The point is: do address the problem (even get professional help if needed), and check that your messages say what you intend them to say, especially in a global context, to people at differing levels of proficiency in English.

In another scenario, the Singapore government has discouraged the use of Singlish in favour of Singapore Standard English. Though many feel that Singlish is a valid marker of Singaporean identity, the government believes that a standard English improves Singaporeans' ability to communicate effectively with other English users throughout the world.

So problems can arise when we take a global perspective. Taking a sample of anglicized words used in Western Europe, we see similar problems. Expressions such as 'a parking' (UK English: a car park; US English: a parking lot) or 'presentation charts' (UK English and US English: presentation slides) are used predominantly in Germany as well as words such as 'handy' in continental Europe (UK English: mobile phone; US English: cellphone) or 'beamer' in France and elsewhere (UK English: projector). But if we are writing globally, by definition, we're not just writing for readers in one country.

Let's look again at that word 'charts' used by many German companies for presentation slides. To a native English reader, the word refers to graphs or tables. If someone says they are preparing some charts to include in their presentation and then e-mails over some slides without any graphs or tables, what am I am likely to assume? That the presentation is complete or incomplete? It will probably be the latter – and valuable time may be lost before I e-mail or telephone that person to ask, 'When I am going to receive the "missing" items?' So here's an instance where quirky use of English can slow down business results simply because it attempts to redefine a standard meaning – and confuses the wider, global audience.

Let's also look again at the words 'handy' for mobile phone or 'beamer' for projector. In these cases, the vast majority of native English speakers are unlikely to have any idea what these words mean. You need to think about how the whole issue impacts on your company, as we'll now see.

# Define business English within your company

My suggestion is this. Do some sort of survey to evaluate whether the terms you use really are understood by your target audience. Terms that are understood in Western Europe may not have the same currency in Asian markets and so on. Just because English-sounding words and expressions have crept into your company usage, this does not mean they are internationally recognized.

Share your findings throughout your company, to gain consensus on how to describe the business English you plan to use. Flag up any words you discover that may not have common currency.

If you have just started your career, you can impress your boss by doing this. You can make a difference, boost your prospects and help your organization shine.

# Your checklist for action

Answer the following questions to help you decide what you could do better:

- Do you communicate with a specific group of English users? Or are you likely to be communicating worldwide?

- Do you identify and then use a single type of English every time you write in English? Or do you need to vary it according to your target audience each time?

- Do you set your computer spellcheck and grammar check to the type(s) of English you use?

- If so, do you check that it does not default to US English spelling (unless that is your preferred variety)?

- Do you regularly check that the words you use are understood by your readers?

- When you do not understand a word, do you feel confident enough to ask its meaning, in order both to understand it and give feedback to the writer?

# Chapter Six
# Writing English for global business

## Looking at how you use English at work

It's useful to hold up a figurative mirror and evaluate as far as is possible:

- how your readers see themselves;
- how you see yourself – and your organization;
- how you see your readers;
- how your readers may see you through your writing.

It's amazing how the images may diverge, and successful writing will take this into account. Its aim will be to remove distortions, bringing the four equally important images together into sharp, correct focus. You can't achieve this focus without appreciating and embracing the fact that different cultures communicate differently. If you are dealing with a particular country, you will naturally need to carry out more detailed research as to the right way to communicate with their culture. The varying channels of social media broaden this need further, as we saw in Chapter 4.

In outline, though, it's true to say that a typical Western style of writing comes over as structured and fairly direct (though a typical British style can have a tendency to waffle).

If we look at Asian cultures, we can find extremely polite, formal, self-effacing communication. It can be considered bad style to get to the point too quickly and rude to make points too directly. So these cultures are less likely to default to a structure considered normal by many, namely, main points, discussion of impact, then further information. Instead they are likely to have a stronger focus on introduction, setting a respectful tone, developing rapport, and then ending on the main points (which they may imply rather than express).

Do take time to think about your cultural writing style for each task. One size won't fit all.

## Do your words say what you think they say?

Have you ever had to explain to readers: 'Oh, I didn't mean that'? If so, you won't be alone.

That's why major UK companies and government agencies, as well as smaller players, all call me in as a troubleshooter to check over their English business writing for the home market too. They ask me to look at the words they use (to internal and external customers, suppliers and so on) in order to help them check their words really say what the companies want them to say. You see, using business English at work isn't just about learning how to write words in English. It's as much about adopting the right frame of mind to make the right connections with readers. You need to stand back and see your writing from all angles. An undoubtedly well-intentioned writer in Australia clearly did not follow this advice when advertising literacy classes, as the text of this poster shows:

Are you an adult that cannot read? If so, we can help you.

The moment you say 'I did not mean that!' is the moment you realize that no, your writing does not add up as you intended. It is not saying the right things.

Writing business English is about reducing verbosity, avoiding misunderstandings and crafting clear, concise messages. But the fewer words you write, the more important it is that you get them right.

# Writing problems faced by non-native English writers

Everybody faces a very real challenge when communicating. How do we convey our precise meaning to others? We all have to work out how to convert what we are thinking into words. When we write, we face additional problems. Are these the right words to put down on paper or on the screen, when we may not be there to explain them to readers?

So many factors can distort our intended meanings, and this book will show you how to avoid many of them. This challenge can be far greater for non-native speakers of English. They have an extra step to overcome: translating their words from their native language into English before they then write them down.

So if as a non-native English speaker you are to write effectively in English, it will be helpful for you to be systematic in approach. A sequence that should help you is this:

1 Identify the thought effectively in your own language.

2 Translate it correctly from your own language into English.

3 You may then need to convert the thought captured in English into the correct written English word.

4 Then make sure that the 'correct written English word' is actually the one that your readers will understand

5 Having done all this, your English writing should enable readers to respond the way you want. That's what you are in business for!

So let's work together to see how you can minimize any distortions. You don't want them interrupting this very important sequence from planning stage through to delivery.

## *Use plain English when you can*

When writing both for the home market and for global business, express the gist of what you are saying in really accessible, plain English. Don't focus on just translating from your own language into English. The more you do this, the worse things can get. Why? Because simply translating can result in:

- over-complicated or incorrect messages;
- focusing on the specific words rather than the overall meaning;
- losing sight of the business need: for example, to write an essential call to action (what to do next).

Choosing unnecessarily complicated words rarely sits well in the modern workplace. It can trap you into choosing 'erudite' over the plainer words 'wise' or 'clever', and you won't be these things if your readers don't understand you! Similarly, think carefully about your readership before writing verbose sentences such as: 'the information we have assembled leads us to believe that...' over: 'we find that'.

Also, don't make assumptions when you translate a word such as 'actualmente' from Spanish to English that it will be the similarly sounding English word 'actually'. The correct word would be 'currently'. Don't guess at meanings, or make your readers have to do the same.

When it comes to calls to action, it's really important to use accessible language. Don't be too preoccupied with getting the English right, as in 'subscribe to our biennial newsletter', to the extent you forget that readers need to see why they should. What's in it for them? Great calls to action use short, persuasive copy in simple language that's easily visible (and often written in a contrasting colour). Click here and 'Get results now' or 'Hurry: today's offer' cannot be overlooked in a way that this verbose sentence (correct though it is) probably would be: 'Why not give her the opportunity to select from our extensive brochure?'

Regularly ask yourself:

- Will my readers recognize the words I use?
- Will they understand their meaning?
- Will these words attract and continue to engage their attention?
- Am I easily enabling the response I need?

## Problems with non-native English writing for native English speakers

Problems that can arise from non-native English (non-NE) writing don't only affect non-NE readers. They impact on native English readers too. Problems include:

- we can't understand some or any of the non-NE writer's writing;
- we almost understand what is meant but don't ask questions as we should (either out of goodwill or because we can't be bothered);
- the wrong meaning then continues to be communicated which can lead to all sorts of problems.

Reading a non-NE writer's approximation to a real English word can, over time, make the native reader begin to accept that word as correct! As an example, I saw 'automisation' written by so many foreign companies over the years that I almost accepted it as real English, even though you won't find it in a dictionary. The trouble is, its inferred meaning isn't actually clear. I thought it was used for 'automation', which can be the case. But very often non-NE writers use it to mean 'computerization'. That's totally different.

Other problems can be:

- Strangely enough (and wrongly, in my opinion), native English speakers sometimes get defensive if their English is corrected by non-NE writers, who can have a very good grasp of English grammar.

- Native English writers and speakers can be unsure whether they should correct non-NE writers who make spelling or grammatical mistakes or whose meanings are unclear.

- Native English writers and speakers can be supremely irritated by one-word or one-line messages that some non-NE writers see as supremely efficient.

- Native English writers and speakers can be equally irritated by over-complicated non-NE writing that has unclear meanings and requires implied rather than stated action.

Knowing that these reactions occur is instrumental in helping you understand not only how to write but also how to seek readers' feedback, to judge how well you are doing. If we are failing our readers, we need to re-design our writing. We need to know the problems first, in order that we can work on the solutions to get it right each time.

If you work in or deal with multicultural teams, make a point of discussing what works and what doesn't. This will bring you all much closer together – and you can design communication that works!

## Problems posed for native and non-native English writers alike

Let's look at some features that can perplex both native English and non-NE writers alike.

## *Idioms, clichés and nuances*

Idioms are expressions that are peculiar to a language, where simply by translating the words, non-natives may be unable to work out what their meanings are. It's true you can feel great mastering some idioms in a foreign language. I feel I am the 'bee's knees'; I am 'over the moon' about it. Do you get the drift of what I am saying, or am I pulling the wool over your eyes? Are you completely puzzled? You could reach for your dictionary but it will take you precious time, so let me explain:

- To be 'the bee's knees' means to be really good, to be excellent.
- 'Over the moon' means delighted.
- 'To get the drift' of something means to get the general meaning.
- 'To pull the wool over someone's eyes' means to deceive them or obscure something from them.

In actual fact, native speakers may also misunderstand idioms: some are quite obscure. Do approach them with caution in business. However competent you may feel in using them, the odds are they will lead to confusion and misunderstanding.

Let's consider clichés now. 'Cliché' has been imported from French into many languages, but, interestingly, it does not always mean the same thing in each. In German, for example, it means a stereotype, whereas in UK English it means a stale expression, something that has been overused to the point that it is ineffective. A cliché often overlaps with corporate jargon or management speak and can undermine a person's writing by making it seem tired.

Here are some examples of clichés, with their meanings shown in brackets:

'In this day and age' (now);

'Pick the low-hanging fruit' (go for the easy option);

'Think outside the box' (think in an original or creative way).

'Nuance' (another word that English has imported from French) means shade or subtlety in language. Unsurprisingly, even native writers can have difficulty understanding nuances. As an example, in one online discussion forum I noticed some English-speaking artists engaged in debate. They were questioning what the differences were between the words tint, hue, shade and so on, when describing aspects of colour. There were many conflicting suggestions and very little consensus. Nuances can be tricky things.

In a business context, let's look at how the subtlety in meaning between 'quite proud' and 'proud' can actually lead to problems. First of all, are you aware that there is a difference in meaning? To a British speaker 'proud' usually has a stronger emphasis than 'quite proud'. If I tell someone I am proud of their work achievements, it's an absolute. They have done very well and I'm telling them that. The moment I say that I am 'quite proud', the perception can be that I'm diluting my pride: I am less proud than I could be. The nuance then implies that the person could have done better.

But very confusingly, I have heard an American boss tell a member of staff that he was 'quite proud' of his achievements. I could hear his intonation in the spoken words. This distinctly told me that he was using 'quite proud' to mean 'very proud'. But we cannot hear intonation in writing (except when we SHOUT through capital letters). So if we use nuances whereby the words persist in meaning different things to different people, these words will not ultimately make commercial sense. So if you can avoid nuances, then why not make life easier, and matters clearer, by doing so?

## Standard and online dictionaries, and the lure of cut and paste

Always check the meanings and spellings of words when unsure. And, whatever you do, don't feel you have to use the most complicated word your dictionary offers.

Let's say you are a non-NE writer using an online dictionary and you type a word in your own language for 'outcome'. You see a selection of English translation words. I tried this in German once and the online dictionary offered, amongst other words, corollary and consecution. Corollary is a word that people may know but would use only in a very specific context. Consecution, though? That is definitely online dictionary-speak!

Non-NE writers can wrongly feel they must choose the most complicated 'intelligent-sounding' choice – which is often the longest – when they come face to face with a bewildering selection of words to choose from. So out goes 'outcome', that almost everyone will understand, and in comes 'consecution'. Is it really an 'intelligent choice' if your readers do not know what you mean?

So we can see how just one wrong word can cause chaos with your meaning. But online dictionaries also ensnare users to use whole phrases where one word would suffice. 'Wow', you may say, 'this is easy, isn't it? And it looks good!' But you need to take context into account too – and maybe adjust your grammar. Some phrases are so specific that if you put them in the wrong place (and this can be a danger with 'cut and paste') your writing becomes nonsense.

I keyed the word 'profits' into one online dictionary and was really amused when it suggested I could use a related phrase: 'the profits of doom'! All right, there may be a global recession, but this is ridiculous. The reference should have been 'prophets of doom', which means people who predict the future and identify hazards ahead. If I were a non-NE writer, I could easily have accepted that this expression exists. Might I not look silly otherwise? I might be seen as not belonging to the club of seasoned professionals who reel off the latest English buzz words. Why put 'my head above the parapet' in order to be 'shot down'?

I think it is rather like the story of the Emperor's new clothes. Someone has to stand up and say 'That's not right!' And it does take self-confidence to do this, which I hope this book will give you in abundance. So do look for the word that people really use. Don't be disappointed if this is more prosaic than the language of Shakespeare. You write intelligently in English for business when your readers understand you.

If there's a particular instance you've encountered, it could be really helpful to jot down this down while the subject is fresh in your mind. Do consider discussing any issues with your boss and colleagues so you can get a fix on how to deal with them.

# Business writing as communication

In business we communicate by speech and writing and visuals. We only succeed if we get our intended message across without distortion.

Here is a very clear example of a distorted message:

> Identifying business writing has to be about messages. Present them you should then in a key that will engage readers' attention – and make them want way to read more.

How did you react to this piece of writing? Did you try to make any sense of it? Did you manage to decode it? Because that is what you would have had to do. And often we find ourselves reading writing that, although not as jumbled as this example, is not far off.

Here is the decoded message:

> Business writing has to be about identifying key messages. You should then present them in a way that will engage readers' attention – and make them want to read more.

You can see how distortion makes a mockery of good advice. So let's now work on identifying the differing ways business readers can react to muddled messages. My findings include these:

- Readers might not be bothered to work out the meaning. Unimpressed, they might walk away from the 'message' – and from the business that it belongs to.

- Such readers might also tell others the bad news.
- Readers might try to work out a meaning: they might decipher it wrongly and do nothing.
- Or they might take the wrong action.
- Readers cannot understand and they need to ask for clarification.
- Readers might be offended and not tell you.
- Readers might complain to you.

Can you see the commercial implications involved in these scenarios? Let's list them here:

- Inaction from readers, or their failure to react the desired way, is bad news.
- Lost custom and goodwill speak for themselves and affect your profits.
- A bad reputation (spread by unhappy readers telling others – especially detrimental when this goes viral as we saw in Chapter 4) can undermine your success and damage your business.
- Being on the receiving end of wrong action is clearly appalling for any business.
- Clarifying messages involves doing the same job twice or more.
- Upsetting readers is never going to be good for any business.
- Complaints may be good news in one sense (you get to hear what your customer thinks, and you can change) but they are also bad news – and they cost you.

---

**Activity:** What problems have you seen at work as a result of distorted messages? Why was that? What 'notes to self' can you jot down?

# English continues to evolve

We're seeing how business writing is in a state of flux and the English language also continues to change. Indeed, modern English has evolved from so many influences: Anglo-Saxon, Latin, Greek, French, Celtic and Dutch and a colonial past. The list goes on. It makes the English very proud of their extremely rich vocabulary, even though they may not have the 22 words for different types of snow that the Eskimos apparently have!

The English used in business today can seem surprisingly informal to many. In France there is an academy dedicated to 'upholding standards' in the way the French language is used. One of its objectives is to keep the language as uncorrupted by outside influences as possible. There is no such English equivalent. However, there is ongoing debate where on one side are those who believe in prescribing rules of traditional grammar etc. On the other are those who believe it is more about examining how language evolves and what is seen as current usage.

That's why you may be puzzled when some English teachers tell you that you can, for example, write 'to boldly go' – thereby splitting the infinitive form of the verb 'to go'. (Some will even dispute whether there is such a thing as an infinitive form in English, as it is not a Latinate language.) Traditional, prescriptive teachers may take a contrary view: don't split the infinitive, write 'to go boldly'.

Feelings can run strongly regarding which of the following is correct:

Understand who are you writing for.

Understand for whom you are writing.

Most people will accept either version (and looking at modern business writing, most would probably write the first), though the prescriptive school will opt for the second. This would be on the basis that (i) 'who' can only be the subject of the sentence (and it isn't here) and (ii) you cannot end a sentence with 'for', as it is a preposition.

So what can you do in view of this dilemma? The advice I give is: reflect the expectations of your target readership, which may involve writing the way your boss or reader expects. Because both English and business writing itself are in a state of flux, sometimes you will find that a middle course is the route to success.

# Non-native English writers can have an advantage!

The most forward-thinking, successful companies where English is not the first language often actively encourage and train employees to perfect the English writing skills they need. A positive learning culture such as this can foster attention to quality and professionalism. It can even result in non-NE staff making more effort than native speakers in avoiding confusion and misunderstandings.

## *Native English writers: beware of complacency!*

Native speakers of any language can assume they are proficient in their own language, so 'of course people understand what we say and write'. But it's not necessarily true. Every company should really assess writing ability when recruiting and/or promoting employees into jobs that need this skill (and, actually, which jobs don't?). Otherwise complacency sets in – and complacency drains the lifeblood of any organization. It's how companies lose the competitive edge.

So let me show you some practical examples where native English writers got it wrong and paid the price.

An upmarket hotel opened its new restaurant, meant to be called *The Brasserie*. Unfortunately, nobody checked the correct spelling of this French word. The restaurant opened to great fanfare. The trouble was, it was called *The Brassiere*. It was not long before it was ridiculed in the national press – but it was long enough for it to lose face (and money on the signage, menus and advertising, all of which had to be redone).

Another unfortunate piece of writing by a native English speaker was this: 'I feel I have become a prawn in the game.' He actually meant to write 'pawn in the game' (using a chess analogy) but the extra letter made a nonsense of this.

So you see it is not just foreigners who make mistakes. But the uplifting fact is that, whatever the nationality, it is virtually always the good who strive to be better!

## Your checklist for action

To use business English at work, your words and the framework that surround them have to be perfect. This is achievable, so why set the bar lower? Maybe it will help to list the stark consequences of getting it wrong:

> Business writing mistakes (including unclear, confusing or alienating messages) can equal lost cash + lost custom + lost goodwill.

For these reasons:

- Make sure that your message is not subordinate to your translation.

- You may be unable to explain things as precisely as you would like, so you may have to focus on the main messages that are essential for readers to know (except for contracts, technical documents etc, where every detail matters!).

- Make sure that you get your message right for your recipient: more complicated text can be counterproductive and confusing for you and your reader.

- If you are preoccupied with correctly describing what you do, you can lose sight of the bigger picture (eg the need to express how you do it better than the rest, to win and retain custom).

- Do the work for your readers: make sure your messages are not losing you (or them) time or money.

- No matter how good our English language skills are, we all need to take the time to check our written English.

- Discuss any points arising from this chapter with colleagues, to flag up any general or specific concerns. This is especially helpful for bringing multicultural teams closer.

# Chapter Seven

# E-mail and instant messaging

## General

In e-mail and instant messaging, the focus is on the one-to-one recipient or the relatively 'captive audiences' of your e-mail thread or address book contacts. It contrasts with social media's main focus on writing to interest and engage a wider (often specifically targeted) audience.

E-mail is a predominant form of business writing today; indeed, inestimable billions of e-mails are sent worldwide each day. Even if we disregard the high percentage of spam that may be filtered out, it's thought that an office worker can spend 28 per cent of a 40-hour working week reading and answering e-mails. Yet few companies offer training or advice on the subject.

Let's look at your business. How many e-mails do you write in a week at work? Do you treat them all as professional, corporate communication? If you hesitate, the chances are that you don't – and if not, why not? Your readers and your competitors may be ahead of you on this. Also, do you check each time you use e-mail that it is the right medium? Would a phone call or face-to-face conversation do the job more effectively?

Poor use of e-mail creates inefficiency in the workplace. We're also losing many traditional problem-solving skills as a direct result as it's easy to pass messages on without dealing with them.

Other factors need to be addressed as well. Non-native and native English writers often write over-concisely at the cost of not making complete sense. And now that an estimated 27 per cent of all e-mails are opened on mobile devices, your well-designed, helpful format may be lost.

The 'on the move' mobile device reader processes information in a different way too: another reason to avoid the beginning, middle and end writing of yesteryear. You have to write smarter than ever before, to get key messages across sooner – yet still remember that everything you write is corporate communication.

# The rise and rise of e-mail

Consumers may be moving away from e-mail to social media and instant messaging but indications are that business e-mail usage will actually increase by 2018 and beyond.

So how do you need to write? Two fundamental findings emerge:

- E-mails are written by virtually all levels of staff in all types of company. Largely gone are the days of the traditional secretary: we mostly have to design our writing ourselves.

- Looking at the statistics, it's easy to see how such vast e-mail usage can lead to information overload. So it's crucial to maintain quality and make things as relevant and easy as possible for the reader, so your e-mails stand out for the right reasons – not because your English or your content is wrong.

# E-mail scenarios to watch out for

## Sending too quickly

We all do it: we type our messages and click on the send button without checking them first. Speed of response can seem like a must but can create particular problems for native and non-native English writers alike. Spelling and grammar mistakes, abrupt tone, overreacting or simply not answering questions can all make readers judge your e-mails in a negative light. Take the time you need to get it right.

## Draft folder

If you are really pressured and know you can't send your e-mail by return, think about drafting a reply. Move it into your draft folder until you can complete it, maybe after asking someone for help.

## CC or cc

This stands for 'carbon copy'. The cc field is for copying your e-mail to other recipients so they see the same message as the main addressee. If you use a cc internally within your company, it's not generally a problem when those listed in the cc field see others' e-mail addresses. But where your cc field includes the e-mail addresses of external recipients, you may get into trouble because of privacy and data protection laws. Spammers can also use these lists – and forwarded e-mail addresses can harbour viruses.

## BCC or bcc

This stands for 'blind carbon copy'. It means that the copy of the e-mail message is sent to a recipient whose address cannot be seen by other recipients. This is useful where confidentiality is required.

# Multi-lingual and other e-mail threads

When it comes to business communication, there is nothing more frustrating, confusing or even downright rude than someone e-mailing you a message you literally cannot understand! Just because you are both corresponding in English, it's not suddenly going to mean that your recipient understands your language. This might seem obvious, yet the widespread use of e-mail threads can make a mockery of this need for clarity.

Read the following e-mail thread starting from bottom to top, to see how a multi-lingual thread can lead to confusion.

---

De: Paul Lederer
À: Harry Brown
Objet: Lead Project A

Hi Harry
Pierre Marceau passed me your request. We've contacted Pilar
Lopez as she's the project manager for this and you'll find her
e-mail on this below.
Kind regards
Paul

-------------------------------------------------------------------

From: Pilar Lopez
To: Paul Lederer
Subject: Lead Project A

Paul,
¡Consigue que me llame!
gracias
Pilar

-------------------------------------------------------------------

De: Paul Lederer
À: Pilar Lopez
Objet: Lead Project A

Pilar,
I think you're probably the best person to deal with the question posed below. Am I right? I know that as you are new to the company, you have difficulty writing in English, so feel free to reply to this in Spanish as I'll understand.
Regards,
Paul

---

De: Pierre Marceau
À: Paul Lederer
Objet: Lead Project A

Paul,
Je n'ai pas les informations dont Harry a besoin. Poux-tu l'aider ?
Merci
Pierre

---

From: Harry Brown
To: Pierre Marceau
Subject: Lead Project A

Hi Pierre,
I understand you have the full brief on this global project and I'm wondering if you could e-mail this over to me for familiarization, please.
Many thanks,
Harry

If I tell you that Harry Brown speaks only English, can you see how unhelpful this thread is going to be? First of all, who is dealing with Harry's request? It seems to be being passed from one person to another but Harry does not know that. The fact that Pilar Lopez has helpfully suggested (in Spanish) that Harry call her, is not something he is going to see from the thread. After all, it's Pierre who understands Spanish, not Harry. Also, why is Pilar suggesting that he give her a call, when he had asked Pierre for details by e-mail?

How is Harry going to feel? Annoyed? Yes. Alienated? Yes. Is the matter resolved? No. Harry will have to make further enquiries. To avoid this alienation (of which the sender is normally unaware, as it's rarely intentional) you could try these alternatives:

- be both courteous and efficient by summarizing, in English, the main facts of the message thread;
- avoid multi-lingual threads altogether;
- start each message afresh.

## Embedding responses

Whether or not you embed responses is a question of knowing how well this method works both for you and your recipients. Some people cannot imagine working any other way. For others it's actually stressful, especially where they are the people left to weave together perhaps five differing views, all embedded into their original e-mail.

Have you ever had to figure out what the overall picture is, at the end of a complicated trail of embedded messages? If you're dealing with messages in your native language it can be quite a challenge. Imagine how much worse this will be where you have to try to interpret broken or variant English too. There comes a point at which embedding messages can become 'hiding messages'. Quit before you get to that point – and start a new e-mail!

This example shows you how tricky it can be to decipher embedded text. Let's say your e-mail asks four people in four different countries for their observations. You suggest they each embed their comments using a different colour. So Alexei in Russia chooses dark blue, Kentaro in Japan chooses teal, Cora in the Netherlands chooses red (and chooses to use capitals as well), and Carmen in Chile chooses brown.

Can you already see the problems that this course of action may present? It's going to become a very complicated procedure. I pity the originator who will have to try to draw the strands together to make sense. Surely it would be simpler to send a separate e-mail to each of the four? Incidentally, can you see why Cora's choice may lead to further complications? I know red is an auspicious colour in China and no doubt in other countries too. But in many countries, red embedded print is used to correct written mistakes or make criticisms. Readers may literally see a comment in red as a problem – even if it's actually meant to be helpful and positive.

Cora has also chosen to use capitals. According to accepted e-mail etiquette, capitals throughout an e-mail signify that you're SHOUTING. Cora's comments could then appear to be criticisms, although she may never realize this or the fact that she might be offending readers as a result. So do evaluate when and how to embed messages and when to avoid this writing technique.

## Structure your e-mails

E-mail is largely viewed as a form of communication that is halfway between conversation and formal business writing. Many people feel this means they can type their ideas:

- in the English words that just occur to them;
- in no particular order;
- with no stated objectives;

- with no attention to punctuation, grammar or any other quality control;
- with no attention to layout.

Yet feedback repeatedly suggests that readers don't like reading solid blocks of text. What's more, if they don't like the look of a piece of writing, they may intuitively feel they are not going to like its content. This feeling can even go so far as to prevent them from bothering to read it.

When it comes to our personal e-mail, and the world of blogging, we can relax to an extent. These are areas where we can let our writing just capture our thoughts, more or less exactly in the English in which they spill out (though we still have to observe the constraints of the law, including libel etc). Readers are more likely to have the time and the inclination to read our outpourings and storytelling – but this approach is definitely best avoided for business e-mail.

My tips apply even more if you are writing English for a cross-cultural audience. Use an easy-to-read font, design good layout and enter some carriage returns when you type, so that your words are not bunched up and difficult to read.

Leave some white space by using paragraphs for new topics; people will thank you for it because, by and large, people like white space. Structure every e-mail to help readers see exactly what your points are and where the e-mail is leading: that is, its purpose and who does what and when.

If you do not make the purpose, the time frame and any call to action clear, then people might not respond. And, of course, if your e-mail has no purpose, then you should not write it!

## Designing how you write e-mails

Here are some guidelines to help you structure your e-mails well.

## Corporate communication

Is there a corporate style regarding layout? Do you have a corporate font? Is the font you use easily readable, such as Arial, Tahoma, and Verdana? Is the point size you use large enough? (12 point or above is often recommended). Don't just use lower case alone: corporate e-mail should still be in standardized English. Are you using your spellcheck and grammar check – and have you selected the correct variety of English?

## Tone and appropriateness

Probably most reader complaints about e-mails relate to poor tone and inappropriate subject matter. Regarding the first point, be aware that you need to introduce the right tone for your target audience in each e-mail, as we have seen earlier.

Check whether you are using the right style of English:

- Is 'Hi' is the right opening salutation?
- Or should you use 'Hello' or 'Dear' followed by the recipient's first name or title and surname?
- Or is it sufficient simply to use their first name alone, for example, 'Paolo'? (Many find this approach curt.)

Most companies I work with do use 'Hi' as the default salutation but this is not a 'one size fits all' solution. When in doubt, using mirroring techniques can be useful in cross-cultural situations. By this I mean that, where feasible, you try replying to readers in a similar way to the way they address you.

Always remember that if you are not prepared to say a particular thing face to face, or if you would not be happy for other people to see your e-mail (including people you may not know about), then do not write it!

## Use a good subject heading; refresh it regularly

If you want people to open your e-mail, write an interesting headline. If it's compelling, so much the better! For instance,

I've just received an e-mail from a company that I've heard of but don't actually know. Their subject heading was: 'Awards & important social media updates'. I opened it. Why? Do you think it was to see what awards they had won? No, it wasn't. The interest for me was to check on the 'important' social media updates. But good for them, they got the reputational message across that they had won awards!

Always think of meaningful subject headings for your readers. 'Update on Project A at end of week 30' is going to be a better heading than simply 'Project A'. In subsequent e-mails refresh the headings, so messages always reflect the current picture wherever possible. How helpful is that heading about week 30 when you're actually discussing progress at week 40?

## Regularly refresh e-mails

I've discussed problems that can arise from multi-lingual e-mail threads. Let me just reinforce the message now: try to get into the habit of stopping e-mail threads, maybe after the third message. Start a new e-mail and if you need to carry information over, just recap the key points.

## Before you send

- Re-read your e-mail and check that your communication in English is correct on every level.
- Make sure it doesn't include previous e-mail threads that may not be appropriate to forward on to the new reader(s).
- Have you included any attachments? Are they in English too?
- If you have copied somebody in, have you explained why?
- Is the subject heading good?
- Is the e-mail easy to read (font style and size etc)?

## *After sending*

Check after the event (a day, two days, a week?) that you have achieved the outcome you want. Check that the English you have written has worked for your needs.

# Instant messaging and texting

Instant messaging (IM) and text messaging (SMS) are some of the fastest growing areas of business communication and are widely used in social media too via services such as WhatsApp, Viber etc.

Both are about messaging that is predominantly text based but instant messaging is more about quick-fire replies between two correspondents (usually within a business). We've seen the problems in sending e-mails too quickly, so it's easy to see how the rapid reply feature of messaging builds in more hazards to avoid!

Around the world, we see something very noticeable in business communication generally as a result. Just take a look at any you have received recently. Even if you work in a highly traditional organization, I bet you'll see abbreviated language, emoticons, and imprecise spellings, grammar and punctuation.

Socially, it's what we expect in this medium, poised as it is somewhere between e-mail and conversation. But it's best to think this through in your workplace. Do you want the increasingly casual style of instant messaging to cross over into your standard business e-mails too?

It's a good point to discuss with colleagues because we're seeing a traditional business e-mail style (see Example 1) change to casual textspeak (see Example 2):

Example 1:

John: Hi. Please may we have a meeting tomorrow?

Jane: Yes, certainly. Shall we say 9.30 am? I look forward to catching up with you.

Example 2:

John: U cool with mtg tom?

Jane: Heyyyy no worries CU tom. 9.30. Catch up then lol

Messaging can be criticized for not having a friendly tone because of the necessary brevity of the form. But this example shows how texting language is often tweaked to convey a friendly feel. The 'u cool' and 'heyyyyy' seems to me friendlier than the 'Hi' and 'I look forward (to it)' and 'yes, certainly' in Example 1.

In Chapter 4 we looked at examples of how instant messaging interaction with customers via social media (regarding complaints, for example), is leading to readers expecting a more conversational style in corporate communication generally.

The pressing need now is how to define its use within your organization. You need to check what is acceptable.

As a first step, understanding the scenarios when texting or instant messaging is going to help your business productivity. Is it something that's essential to update people on crisis management, project status, orders, complaints, journey delays, meetings and other time-sensitive matters where deadlines are critical? If you have a few seconds free that can be a most effective use of time – and we've also seen in Chapter 4 how speed of response matters when dealing with customers via instant messaging on social media.

On a very practical level, just as you need to think about your readers' proficiency in English in other writing tasks, don't forget this equally applies in the fast-moving messaging arena. Just because you may be able to fire off let's say five points – if not simultaneously, at least in quick succession – doesn't mean your correspondent can reply as speedily.

Have you personally ever seen the 'wrong answers' coming in from your respondent – in the sense that they don't align sequentially with your questions? Far from messaging providing the solution, it creates the problem! It's just as important to write effectively in texts and IM as in any other form of writing. Try one question at a time and allow adequate time for the reply you need to arrive.

Instant messaging and texting can also create the same sort of barriers as other jargon does. LOL is frequently used and can be taken to mean both 'Laugh out loud' or 'Lots of love'. Can you see the problems when abbreviations can perhaps unintentionally embarrass people into having to admit they actively don't like it or find it inappropriate? They can equally be embarrassed by not understanding it – or having to pretend that they do. So tread with care.

Here are some tips to help:

- Consider a business user policy that's separate from your personal use and which can include status/availability settings (within the system application you use) and whether you use texting and messaging for internal and external use.

- As part of this policy, consider whether sensitive or negative information can or should ever be relayed by this method rather than face to face or by formal notification.

- Remember that all written messages can provide an audit trail. Be professional: project company values and quality – and maintain reputation (yours and others').

- Work out which expressions have common currency so readers understand any shorthand you use.

- If you do use emoticons and emojis (small digital icons that signify feelings) only use those that are right for your reader. For example, the 'thumbs up' sign expresses positivity to some cultures but is offensive to others. Also be aware that not all devices will display the emoticons yours does.

- Keep texting and messaging only for quick response, not for the detail.

- As with e-mail, don't let speed trap you into inferior writing. Abbreviated spelling may be acceptable but each message has to be both organized and understood.

- Observe etiquette: just because you are free for those seconds, you might be interrupting someone else's meeting etc, even if their status setting indicates they are available. Ask when they can reply if you don't hear by return.

- Etiquette also involves the right tone – and understanding recipients' preferred style.

- As with e-mail, let readers know where the message is leading and what response you need.

- It may be better to deal with one message at a time because of the 'on the go' nature of the medium. Use line breaks to avoid run-on sentences that are difficult to decipher.

- Check whether texting or messaging mode is migrating into your other business communication and what guidelines you may need to have in place to uphold quality and values.

**Activity**: Discuss the best use of texting and instant messaging with colleagues and how this may impact on your other corporate communication. Collaborate on the code you will use to avoid misunderstandings, even offence. It's also helpful to decide on the salutations/endings you will use (as required). You might be surprised how important this is in workplaces to avoid irritated readers' faces!

# Your checklist for action

Before you press send, ask yourself:

- Is e-mail or instant messaging the right communication medium? Is your English fit for purpose? E-writing is corporate communication and your English has to be professional.

- Have you made the e-mail subject heading relevant so people want to/ know they must read it?

- In exchanges, have you refreshed your headings (if appropriate) and updated details that have changed?

- Did you get to the point in accessible language so readers know where you are leading?

- Did you systematically read and cover the points in the e-mail or message to which you are replying?

- Have you done a spellcheck and grammar check on your e-mails, using the correct variety of English?

- Have you overreacted? If you are not prepared to say your message face to face or let it be seen by others, you should not send it.

- Would it be a problem for you or your organization if this e-mail or message is forwarded in its entirety to other people without your knowledge? Don't forget that all written messages can be used in an audit trail.

- Are you sending the attachments you promised?

- If you are copying someone in, have you explained why?

- Have you developed the right rapport with your readers and met their business and cultural expectations?

- Have you checked your meanings?

- Have you set (and are you remembering to update) your IM status?
- Check whether messaging mode is migrating into your other more formal business communication and what guidelines you may need to have in place to uphold quality and values.

# Chapter Eight
# Punctuation and grammar tips

## Why punctuation and grammar matter

This extract shows what unpunctuated writing looks like:

> mr jones the companys hr director called mrs smith into his office
> for an update on the latest recruitment drive he wanted to know
> whether the online application system was working reports had
> filtered through that all was not going to plan mrs smith explained
> that candidates were certainly experiencing problems as the
> systems had crashed in her opinion it would be better to extend the
> closing date would he be prepared to authorize this

Did you have any problem deciphering this? A lot of people will
find it difficult. If we write poetry we may actively want people
to work out meaning. We may even want them to create their
own meaning; but this should not apply to business writing!

In writing, punctuation is an aid that helps our readers to
understand our messages. The extract could be punctuated a
number of ways. I will use one way to show how it becomes
easier to read:

> Mr Jones, the company's HR director, called Mrs Smith into his
> office for an update on the latest recruitment drive. He wanted to
> know whether the online application system was working. Reports
> had filtered through that all was not going to plan.

Mrs Smith explained that candidates were certainly experiencing problems as the systems had crashed. In her opinion, it would be better to extend the closing date.

Would he be prepared to authorize this?

You see, punctuation and grammar are aids that help writing to be understood and help us to communicate clearly. Whether you are a native or non-native English speaker, you may find some aspects challenging. Bosses really do (or should) prefer you to ask a line manager or a mentor if you are unsure. They absolutely should offer support to people with dyslexia or other writing challenges too. Top entrepreneur Richard Branson is dyslexic yet writes best-selling business books and much-admired blogs, as we have seen. He openly says he relies on one of his right-hand men to check his English before he publishes because he knows that this matters. That's such an inspirational message. The best leaders encourage supportive teamwork so that companies get things right on all levels.

So, all the topics in this chapter are an essential component in the Word Power Skills writing system. When you have a good grasp of the principles, you will feel secure in the knowledge that your sentences will work because you have designed them to work. And if you are not sure about something, you will have the confidence to ask for help.

# Punctuation and other marks

English terms and symbols used to describe punctuation marks are:

capital letters or upper case: A, B, C

lower case: a, b, c

comma: ,

full stop (UK English) or period (UK and US English) or

dot: .

speech or double quotation marks or inverted commas: " "

speech or single quotation marks or inverted commas: ' '

question mark: ?

exclamation mark: !

apostrophe: '

hyphen or dash: –

slash or stroke: /

brackets: ( )

square brackets: [ ]

ampersand: &

'at' sign: @

colon: :

semicolon: ;

asterisk: *

# Parts of speech and other grammar

## Parts of speech

In English grammar, words are categorized into what we term parts of speech. These include nouns, pronouns, adjectives, verbs, adverbs, prepositions, conjunctions and interjections.

A noun names a person, place or thing. For example:

girl, London, newspaper;

The man drank his coffee.

A pronoun is a word that can take the place of a noun and functions like it. For example:

I, this, who, he, they;

There's Peter, who won the lottery.

Notice how the noun 'Peter' became the pronoun 'who' within the same sentence.

An adjective is a word that describes a noun. For example:

red, lovely, clever;

That is a lovely photo.

A verb is a 'doing word' or describes a state of being. For example:

write, run, work, be;

She is an assistant who works hard.

Sometimes a verb needs two or three words to complete it. For example:

I am working in Moscow this week.

You will be travelling first class.

An adverb is a word that describes a verb. For example:

fast, happily, later, urgently;

The project manager always delivered on time.

In that last example there is an adverb, 'always', and an adverbial phrase, 'on time' which describe the verb 'delivered'.

A preposition is a word that links a noun to another noun. For example:

to, on, under, in;

Please put the papers on the desk.

A conjunction is a word that joins words or sentences. For example:

and, but, or, so;

I need a flipchart but that is all.

An interjection is a short exclamation, often followed by an exclamation mark (!). For example:

hi! oh!

## Some other grammatical points of interest

Commas can separate one group of words in a sentence from another so that the meaning is clear. You will see how they flag up different meanings in these two sentences:

Sanjay, our vice-president has left the company.

Sanjay, our vice-president, has left the company.

In the first sentence, the writer is telling Sanjay that their vice-president (somebody else) has left the company. In the second sentence, the writer is telling somebody (whose name is unknown to us) that Sanjay (who is the vice-president) has left the company.

In order to use commas correctly, it helps to know that a comma signifies a brief pause. Very often, people wrongly use a comma to do the work of a full stop (period). For example:

I examined the computer, it had obviously been damaged.

As there are two complete statements here, not just a pause, we could try a full stop: 'I examined the computer. It had obviously been damaged.' However, this sounds rather stilted and a native English writer is likely to use a conjunction to add fluidity. For example: 'I examined the computer and found it had obviously been damaged.'

A comma is also used to link lists of items, groups of words, adjectives, actions and adverbs. For example:

She listed, there and then, the things she would need for her presentation: a laptop, a projector, screen, flipchart and marker pens.

Apostrophes show where one or more letters have been left out of a word. For example:

I'm = contraction of 'I am';

It's = contraction of 'it is' or 'it has';

You'll = contraction of 'you will'.

Apostrophes can also show possession or ownership. For example:

The student's rights = the rights of one student;

The students' rights = the rights of students.

The general rule is:

apostrophe before the s ('s ) = singular possession;
apostrophe after the s (s') = plural possession.

Unfortunately, English always has some irregular forms, such as:

men = plural of man; but the possessive is men's;
children = plural of child; but the possessive is children's;

its = possessive of it – yet takes no apostrophe at all!

## Forming plurals of nouns

As you will know, most nouns have a singular form (to denote one) and a plural (to denote more than one). There are exceptions that I have highlighted earlier, such as training and information. The standard way of forming plurals from singular nouns is to add 's'. However, this does not always work, as in the case of 'child, children', 'lady, ladies', 'foot, feet', to mention a few. So do refer to a mainstream English grammar book if you need more help with this.

There is one point that I would like to address here, as it arises so often. It concerns the wrong use of an apostrophe followed by 's' to signify a plural meaning. For example, 'tomato's' and 'company's'. The correct plurals are 'tomatoes' and 'companies'.

**Activity:** Do you or your colleagues find any aspects of punctuation and grammar a challenge? It's well worth jotting down any points you feel you could work on individually, or as teams.

## Vowels and consonants

In written English, 'a, e, i, o, u' are the standard vowels. The remaining letters in the alphabet are consonants.

## The definite and indefinite article

The word 'the' is called the definite article and has the same form in singular and plural. The words 'a' and 'an' are known as the indefinite article and only exist in the singular. For the plural, English uses the word 'some'.

If as a non-native English writer you're sometimes confused about when to use the definite or indefinite article, you are definitely not alone. A general guideline to help is this: when you're referring to something in general, use 'a' before a word beginning with a consonant or 'an' before a word beginning with a vowel. (Once again though, true to form, English has exceptions: some native speakers would say 'an hotel'.)

Here is an example of 'a' in this usage:

Cheese for sale: six euros a kilo, *not* 'six euros the kilo', as many non-NE writers would expect.

As an interesting aside, note that in English, goods are described as being 'for sale'. Some cultures express it the reverse way: 'to buy'. English speakers would say and write 'House for sale', not 'House to buy'.

Let's say a company receives this e-mail: 'Please can you let me know how long an order will take to deliver?' The company will view the question posed as tentative – and thus non-specific. There is no order, only a general enquiry about how long it would take if somebody did place an order. Now let's say the company receives this enquiry: 'Please can you tell me how long the order will take to deliver?' The word 'the' makes this enquiry far more specific. The question is more likely to relate to an order that has been placed.

# Paragraphs

Paragraphs help your reader understand the organization of your writing because each paragraph is a group of sentences about a topic. Your key messages become easy to identify and the format makes it easy for you to develop them. Paragraph headings (and sub-headings, such as we so often see on the web) are increasingly used to signpost messages and highlight structure for readers' ease.

## Brackets, bullet points and dashes

Use these to break up text (especially if it's rather lengthy) so your reader is not overwhelmed, and you can also use commas, as I am doing here, to make a longish sentence more manageable.

On the reverse side, too many short sentences can seem abrupt. So to keep your writing interesting, try mixing and matching these features to vary and enhance your style.

# Verbs and tenses

You are likely to have been taught the finer points of English grammar at school, in college or by self-study. Entire books are written on this extensive subject and it's beyond the scope of this handbook to go into any great detail. But here's an outline as a refresher.

As you saw, a verb is a 'doing' word. It can consist of one or more words. The infinitive of a verb is the base form, for example 'to work', 'to give', 'to do'.

The present participle is formed by adding '-ing' to the infinitive. The 'to' part is dropped. This construction is then used with the verb 'to be' to form what are known as continuous tenses. For example: 'They are working.'

If the infinitive ends in 'e' ('to give', 'to come') the general rule is to drop the 'e' when adding the '-ing'. For example: 'He is giving', 'They are coming'.

The past participle is normally formed by adding '-ed' to the infinitive. Again, the 'to' part is dropped. This construction is used with the verb 'to have' to form perfect (completed past) tenses. For example: 'The train has departed,' 'The post has arrived.'

Irregular verbs form the perfect differently, so do refer to grammar sources if you're unsure. Examples are: 'It has grown' (not grow-ed), 'The time has flown by' (not fly-ed).

## Tenses

The simple tenses in English are the starting point for global business writing today.

The present tense has the same form as the infinitive (except the verb 'to be'). When the subject is 'he', 'she', 'it' or a noun, English adds '-s' or '-es'.

To form the future tense, English adds 'will' (or 'shall' – though this is less frequently used now).

To form the past tense, '-ed' is normally added to the infinitive.

(Once more though, a word of caution: there are many irregular verbs where this doesn't work!)

A regular example is:

verb: to work (regular verb)

simple present tense:
- I work
- you (singular and plural) work
- he, she, it works
- we work
- they work

simple future tense:
- I, you (singular and plural), he, she, it, we, they will work

simple past tense:
- I, you (singular and plural), he, she, it, we, they worked

There are naturally many more tenses that you will need to study in depth and dedicated grammar resources will help you. That said, there is one tense that seems to present a real workplace problem that businesses often ask me about. It is the present continuous tense.

This is formed by using the present tense of 'to be' with the present participle of the verb in question. Let's say I want the present continuous tense of 'to write'. The forms are:

I am writing

you (singular and plural) are writing

he, she is writing

we are writing

they are writing

The question I'm so often asked is: when do we use the present continuous rather than the present tense? The answer is in three parts:

- When the action is taking place now ('I am writing this sentence at this very moment.').

- When the action is taking place now but also is carrying on into the future ('I am writing this book at this very moment – but also over the coming months.').

- When the action is planned for the future ('I am writing another book next year.').

With regard to this last sentence, the future tense would also be correct, namely: 'I will write another book next year.'

We use the present tense for more general actions or states that have no particular time reference. For example:

We drink water to survive.

If I find a mistake, I correct it.

Non-native English writers can be confused about when to write, for example:

She lives in Tokyo.

She is living in Tokyo.

Both are correct – but the second version often implies to a native English speaker that 'She is living in Tokyo (at the moment).'

# Agreement of subject and verb

When a subject in a sentence is in the singular, then the verb must be in the singular too. When the subject is plural, then the verb is in the plural, in agreement with it. This is also called concord. Examples are:

Paul is at university and so is his brother.

Paul is at university and so are his brother and sister.

They understand the reason why they have to do this.

She understands the reasons why she has to do this and why you have to do it too.

These conditions apply now.

This condition applies now.

Non-NE writers can forget to check concord in their writing. A typical example is:

Sara has received our e-mail. Has you received it too? Correct version: Sara has received our e-mail. Have you received it too?

As a rule of thumb, simply work out who is doing the action and make your verb relate to who or what is doing it. In some sentences you may have to refer back to check.

Incidentally, there are certain words in English where it is possible to use a singular word in a plural sense too. Examples are: government, council, committee, company.

So in UK English, you can write:

The government is changing the law on this.

The government are changing the law on this.

The reasoning behind this is that these nouns can be viewed as entities by themselves or as bodies of people. On this track, another often-used word comes to mind. This is the word 'staff', where it means personnel. It is used as a singular in US English but exists only in the plural in UK English. So UK English says: 'The staff are taking a vote on this.' US English says: 'The staff is taking a vote on this.'

## Question tags

These are used a lot in English conversation, and non-NE speakers can find them quite hard to master. As they are now used in workplace writing too, here are some tips.

Speakers and writers use question tags to encourage their listeners or readers to respond. It helps check that people agree or understand what you are saying or writing.

Examples are:

It's a good outcome, isn't it?

You don't have a meeting today, do you?

You can make it in time, can't you?

Examples of incorrect usage would be:

You have got the right files, isn't it?

He is wrong, doesn't he?

These kind of things are dealt with in your department, isn't it?

Correct versions of these would be:

You have got the right files, haven't you?

He is wrong, isn't he?

These kinds of things are dealt with in your department, aren't they?

Tips to help you:

Try balancing the same verb (including whether it is singular or plural) on either side of the sentence.

Then use a negative in the end questioning part of the sentence.

## Open and closed questions

When you write English across cultures, do be aware that closed questions typically lead to a yes/no/factual answer.
Examples are:

Please can you complete this report by month end?

Is the presentation ready?

If you are dealing with a reserved culture, it could be a better idea to use an open question, such as:

Please could you give an indication of when you can complete this?

What do you think?

The recipient then has to give a fuller and informative answer.

# Comparison

## Comparison of adjectives

In English, adjectives can have three degrees: positive, comparative and superlative.

The positive is just the usual form of the adjective; for example: a happy child, a large book, a comfortable chair.

The comparative is used in comparing one thing or group with another; for example: the shorter of the two brothers; ponies are smaller than horses.

If it is a short word, we normally form the comparative by adding '-er'.

The superlative is used when comparing one thing or group with more than one other; for example: she is the oldest of the three sisters; that is the greatest suggestion yet.

If it's a short word, we normally add '-est' to the positive.

Adjectives of three syllables or more and most adjectives of two syllables form their comparative by placing the word 'more' before the adjective. They form the superlative by placing 'most' in front of the adjective.

Some adjectives have quite different words for the comparative or superlative. For example:

good, better, best;

many, more, most;

little, less, least.

A common mistake is where writers use the superlative where they should be using the comparative. For example: 'That is the best of the two offers' is, strictly speaking, wrong. It should be: 'That is the better of the two offers.' There would have to be three or more offers for 'best' to be correct. Similarly, instead of 'She is the youngest of the two employees', the correct version would be 'She is the younger of the two employees.'

## Comparison of adverbs

Short adverbs are compared in the same way as adjectives:

soon, sooner, soonest;

fast, faster, fastest.

With adverbs of two syllables or longer, you usually form the comparative and superlative by adding 'more' and 'most' to the positive degree of the word:

carefully, more carefully, most carefully;

easily, more easily, most easily.

Once again, English often comes up with irregular forms:

badly, worse, worst.

well, better, best.

# Fluidity in writing

Fluidity when writing English for business pays great dividends: you provide the links so that the reader does not have to work them out. This next example illustrates how.

> ABC Ltd is a well-established manufacturing company founded in 2008 that has decided to go for growth in its next five-year plan.
>
> **Despite** a downturn in the manufacturing sector generally, ABC has identified two principal ways of maintaining a successful business.
>
> **First**, management has changed the structure of the business by splitting its commercial department into two entities: sales and production. **Second**, it has introduced a new outcome-based approach to assessment, which involves staff to a greater degree than before.
>
> **As a result**, the company has significantly improved profits **as well as** winning a prestigious customer service award.

# Your checklist for action

- Present facts clearly and present a well-argued, well-supported business case.

- Write so that readers don't have to make an effort to understand you or come back to you for further information, or wait for you to make things clear.

- Write so that readers are more likely to take a favourable view of you.

- Punctuation serves the useful purpose of helping readers read messages; and it highlights where the emphasis needs to go.

- Grammar helps you set out business writing into manageable sections that help readers understand your meaning.

- Identify areas of punctuation and grammar to work on; do ask for support, if needed.

- Fluidity helps you set out the points in a coherent way. All the points you make add up. Two and two are seen to make four in your writing, not just in your sums.

# Chapter Nine
# Writing tips for everyday business

## Writing a date

### Differing conventions

There are a number of correct ways of writing dates in English. The UK English format (which most of Europe uses) is:

DD/MM/YY, where D = day, M = month, Y = year.

This contrasts with the US format, which is:

MM/DD/YY.

And both are in contrast with the format used in Japan, for example, which is:

YY/MM/DD.

Not understanding the different conventions can create immense problems. If you have to book international transport or hotel accommodation, or arrange deliveries, meetings and so on, you'll know how important it is to input the correct dates. It can simply be a question of house style regarding the format you choose to be your default convention. However, you may need to be flexible and understand that customers may be using a different convention. Check if there's any uncertainty. Sometimes be prepared to mirror their convention, as long as it's an acceptable version that makes sense. Being in business should be about embracing customers' needs, not about seeing them as 'awkward' if they do something differently.

Examples that are all perfectly acceptable in UK English are:

21 January 2018;

21st January, 2018;

21 Jan 2018;

21st Jan 2018;

21/01/18.

If your house style uses the format '1st, 2nd, 3rd', you may have spotted that the abbreviation is based on the spoken or written version of the word in question. So 1st stands for 'first', 2nd for 'second', 3rd for 'third', and so on – placing the final two letters of the abbreviated word behind the number.

As I mentioned, US English uses a month/day/year format, as do some other countries. In this case, you would write:

January 21 2018;

01/21/18.

This particular date isn't too problematic because we know that there are not 21 months in a year. But where readers don't understand the differences between the UK and US conventions, they could have problems with a date such as 03/06/18. In the UK this denotes 3 June 2018, but in the United States it denotes 6 March 2018.

## International date format

This was devised to make the way we write dates internationally understandable. It is based on the following format:

YYYY – MM – DD.

In this format, YYYY refers to all the digits (eg 2019), MM refers to the month (01 to 12) and DD refers to the day (01 to 31).

When there is any doubt, it's really useful to write your dates in English this way.

## Some confusions

### Days and weeks

If you write 'next Tuesday', people can get confused as to whether you're referring to the first Tuesday that follows after the day you wrote this – or whether you mean a Tuesday in another week. So, as an example, if you write it on a Monday, is 'next Tuesday' the following day (which I would take it to mean), or the Tuesday of the following week? If you write it on a Friday, it is easier to see that it would have to be the Tuesday of the following week.

'This coming Tuesday' has the same meaning as 'next Tuesday'. So do be careful. I know of instances where misunderstandings about this have led to missed appointments. Ironically, the people who misunderstand the correct use of the expression are the ones who can get angry. Also, imagine the cost if you book foreign travel for the wrong date. The best arrangement is always to write the precise date you mean, for example: 'next Tuesday, 4th November'.

'In a couple of weeks' literally means 'in two weeks', as 'couple' means 'two' in English. It is true that 'a couple of weeks' can be used in a looser sense, meaning in about two weeks, but it's best to check. As another example, the Dutch expression '*paar dagen*' means a few days, but the Dutch often wrongly translate this into English as 'a couple', or 'two' days. So where orders are concerned, it's always best to clarify what is meant.

'Next Monday week' means 'a week from next Monday'. 'Over a week' in English means 'in more than a week's time'. But non-NE writers often use the expression 'over a week' to mean in a week's time, that is, one week from now. An example would be: 'The delivery will be over a week.' Again be careful if you are dealing with orders, because you can confuse.

'A fortnight' means two weeks. I find that many nationalities are unaware of this word, so it can be better to avoid it.

'A long weekend' means a break of three or four days that includes a Saturday and Sunday, and may start on a Friday and end on the following Monday.

## Time off

In UK English, people usually refer to their 'holidays', where US English uses 'vacation'. Time off work for holidays is referred to as 'leave'; time off through illness is 'sick leave'; parents' time off from work when a baby is born is either 'maternity leave' (for the mother) or 'paternity leave' (for the father).

Time off work may be 'paid leave' or 'unpaid leave', depending on circumstances.

## Public and bank holidays

A public holiday is an official holiday for the majority of a state or country. In the UK, the term 'bank holiday' is used when the public holiday falls on a weekday when banks are closed by law.

When you write about public holidays or bank holidays globally, be aware that they can vary from country to country, usually being cultural in origin.

# Time

Things can go seriously wrong when different nationalities fail to understand that they may have differing conventions for writing times. People fail to turn up to meetings at the right time, they miss flights, deadlines... in short, if a matter is time bound it can go wrong. And what in business is not linked to time? Here are some guidelines to help.

## *UK English*

All these written versions are correct in English:

The meeting starts at 09.00.

The meeting starts at 9am (or 9 am or 9 a.m.).

The meeting starts at nine o'clock in the morning.

The meeting starts at nine in the morning.

English usage includes both the 12-hour clock (morning and afternoon) and the 24-hour clock (especially for timetables), so:

09.00 means nine o'clock in the morning;

21.00 means nine o'clock in the evening.

Strangely enough, 24.00 is also 0.00 hours!

If we write in English, 'The meeting starts at half past eight', this could mean 'The meeting starts at 08.30 or 20.30.'

Often we'll know from context which is correct. For example, if meetings are held during normal office hours, then half past eight in the morning is the more likely time. But say we work in a staggered-hours environment, then it could be a morning or an evening meeting. You need to clarify.

## *Differing conventions in different countries*

Mishaps or missed meetings and other appointments all arise when we fail to realize that the way different countries express time isn't standard. For example, the United States does not generally use the 24-hour clock (except specifically by some professions: for example, the military, the police, the medical profession). Some countries (such as Germany and the Netherlands) use a format to express half an hour before an hour. This is alien to native English writing – where half past six, for example, should be expressed as 'half seven' to the German or Dutch way of thinking.

Don't underestimate how problematic failing to appreciate this source of misunderstanding can be. Do ensure that everyone understands how to write and read times in English, for the sake of efficiency.

# Numbers

If you are writing numbers in English, also be aware that different nationalities may interpret the numbers differently. Look how your order books – and your bottom line – could be affected. For example, the words 'billion' and 'trillion' can have completely different meanings in the UK, Germany, France and the United States.

But a zillion means a large indeterminate number, so that expression at least is standard!

A fairly old imperial expression you will still find on occasion is dozen. It means 12.

You use a comma when you write a number comprising four or more digits. Counting from right to left, you place the comma after each three digits:

1,000;

10,000;

100,000;

100,000,000.

## How the decimal point is written in English

'Decimal point' is the UK English term for the dot placed after the figure that represents units in a decimal fraction: for example, 9.6.

This may differ from the way you express the decimal point in your language. You may be used to using a comma – for example 9,6 – or you may express 100,000,000 as 1000.000.000. It's not overly confusing but it's best to be aware of this difference when you write in English.

## Decimal points when writing monetary units in English

Some nationalities express their decimal currencies using commas where there is a decimal fraction: €1,80.

If you are writing a tariff in English, you express this amount as: €1.80

Other punctuation differences are apparent in the following written representation of the same number. The UK English version is the first of these:

890,123.50

890.123,50

# Measurements

Do you have to write measurements in English? If you're writing globally, do be aware that different countries use different systems. Broadly speaking, these are called metric and imperial.

The United States largely uses imperial and the UK and other countries may use a combination. You will need to research if you're involved in orders that use either system. To give you an idea, some differences are as follows:

Metric system:

- length: centimetre, metre, kilometre (US spelling: meter etc);
- weight: gram, kilogram, tonne;
- capacity: millilitre (ml), litre (US spelling liter etc);
- temperature: Centigrade or Celsius.

Imperial system:

- length: inch, foot, yard, mile;
- weight: ounce, pound, ton;
- capacity: fluid ounce, pint, gallon;
- temperature: Fahrenheit.

Even within the imperial system, you'll find that a US ton is not the same as a UK ton, and a US gallon is different to a UK gallon. Temperatures are also written using different systems:

Centigrade or Celsius: freezing point of pure water 0° (degrees); boiling point 100°;

Fahrenheit: freezing point of pure water 32°; boiling point 212°.

# Your checklist for action

- When writing dates, times and measurements, one size doesn't fit all.
- Understand the conventions your readers use.
- If you don't do this, you may miss appointments, delivery deadlines etc.
- Your order books may be adversely affected if you get dates, times and numbers wrong – your profits too.
- Write as precisely as possible to avoid misunderstandings: for example, 2nd January 2018.

# Chapter Ten
# Common confusions and how to avoid them

## Common confusions for both NE and non-NE writers

Some words repeatedly cause businesses confusion. In many cases it's because different people within the same company set their computer spellcheck to different varieties of English. Often homonyms confuse. These are words that have the same sound but can have different meanings and spellings.

### *Words or spellings that commonly confuse*

Here are some commonly confused words, together with examples of correct usage.

### Receive and recieve

The correct version is 'receive'. A useful rule in English spelling is that after the letter 'c' the letter 'e' goes before 'i'.

### Stationary and stationery

'Stationary' means standing still: for example, 'The careless driver crashed into a stationary car.'

'Stationery' means writing and printing materials: for example, 'I have ordered new business stationery for my office.

## Licence and license, practice and practise

In UK English, the nouns relating to these words end in '-ce'. The verbs end in '-se'. For example:

> Which doctor's practice do you go to? (Practice = noun = the doctor's place of work.)

> You should practise what you preach. (Practise = verb.)

In US English it's completely different. 'Practice' (note the *c*) and 'license' (note the *s*) are always the spellings, no matter whether they are nouns or verbs. For example:

> He has a valid license (noun), so he is licensed (verb) to drive here.

> The best practice (noun) is to practice (verb) what you preach.

## Remember and remind

'To remember' means to be able to bring something or someone back into your mind. For example: 'I must remember to update those details' (meaning: nobody else is involved).

'To remind' means to cause or prompt someone to remember something. For example: 'Please remind me to update those details.'

## Compliment and complement

'Compliment' is a noun or verb meaning praising or admiring.

'Complement' is a noun or verb meaning a thing that completes something else. For example:

> We are always delighted to receive a compliment from a customer. When dining, the right ambience complements the meal.

## Loose and lose

'Loose' is an adjective that means not tightly packed or fixed. For example: 'There is a loose connection in the wiring system.'

'Lose' is a verb that means cease to have, be unable to find. For example: 'If we lose their parcel we will also lose their custom.'

## There and their

'There' is an adverb meaning in that place.
'Their' is an adjective meaning belonging to them. For example:

The file you need is over there.

It will be their turn next.

## Where, were and we're

'Where' is an adverb, meaning in (or to) which place, direction or respect.
'Were' is a verb, the past tense of 'to be'.
'We're' is a contraction of 'we are'. For example:

Where are we going on holiday? You were at home last night and now you are at work. We're attending a training course today.

## Your and you're

'Your' means belonging to you.
'You're' is the contraction of you are. For example:

Your bag is in the other room.

You're expected in half an hour.

## May and can

The verb 'can' in English is used to express ability or being allowed to do something. It is definite in meaning. For example:

I can speak Spanish = I am able to speak Spanish.

Juan's boss says he can have a day off – Juan's boss says he is allowed to have a day off.

The verb 'may' is used to express possibility. For example, 'I may learn Spanish or Mandarin Chinese but haven't decided yet' tells us that the speaker is not yet able to speak either language.

'May' is also used to ask permission in a polite way: for example, 'May I go with you?' or 'May I have a cup of coffee, please?' That said, it is quite normal for business peers to say or write 'Can we talk about this?', 'Can I attend the meeting?'

## Should, must and have to

'Should', 'must' and 'have to' are verbs that convey obligation. In writing 'should' can be interpreted as weaker in meaning than 'must' or 'have to'. For example, if I write, 'You should always check your spelling before you send an e-mail' you might think I am just recommending this as good practice. You could see it as an option, not an obligation. On the other hand, if I write, 'You must always check your spelling before you send an e-mail', then I'm making it very clear that this is not an option; it is a directive. 'Have to' carries the same weight.

## Borrow and lend

If you 'borrow' something you take and use something that belongs to someone else (on the understanding that you will return it). For example: 'As it's raining, please may I borrow your umbrella? I'll give it back to you tomorrow.'

If you 'lend' something you give something to someone else to use (on the understanding that they will return it). For example: 'Has your pen broken? I'll lend you mine until you get a new one.' So you would be wrong to write: 'I need to write but my pen has broken. Can I lend yours?' The pen is not yours to give to someone else! You need to borrow it in order to use it.

## Teach and learn

When someone teaches, they give knowledge or instruction about a subject to someone else. For example: 'I am teaching you some tips about writing English for business.'

When someone learns, they receive knowledge or instruction. For example: 'You are learning how to improve your writing.' So you would be wrong to write: 'Will you learn me how to write?' You are the only person who can carry out the act of learning! I can show you how you will learn, by teaching you.

# Acronyms

Acronyms make an abbreviated word formed by the initial letters of other words or a compound noun. The idea is to make the subject easier to refer to and easier to remember.

When you use abbreviations and acronyms, write them in full at the first mention, then follow with the abbreviation in brackets: for example, Regional Development Agency (RDA). People tend not to do this when an acronym is very likely to be recognized internationally. An example would be the UN (United Nations). It does depend on your target audience. After that first explanation, you may just use the acronym in the text that follows.

I once received an e-mail referring to APAC populations. I imagined that the writer was referring to Asia Pacific populations... but decided to see if there were other acronyms for APAC. There certainly are! I will list just some:

APAC: Asia and Pacific;

APAC: Asia Pacific Advisory Committee;

APAC: All People Are Customers;

APAC: Atlantic Pilotage Authority Canada.

Each group will no doubt have it that their target audience will, 100 per cent, understand their acronym. But my experience as a consultant tells me otherwise!

**CASE STUDY**   How an unexplained acronym created problems.

A director was giving a presentation at a large multinational company recently. One slide, entitled 'BHAGs', was beamed across the hall and, without explaining the acronym, the director spoke enthusiastically on a ground-breaking vision for the company.

After a while, he asked if anyone had any questions. A hand went up, and one brave employee asked: 'What is a BHAG?' pronouncing the word as 'bag'.

'You don't know what a BEE-hag is?' asked the director, noticeably surprised. The questioner probably felt embarrassed. 'Would anyone like to explain?' continued the director. There was silence from the floor. It seemed that nobody could be actually sure what the acronym stood for. Certainly nobody volunteered to explain so it was likely that the questioner was not the only one not to understand.

For the record, BHAG (pronounced bee-hag) stands for 'Big, hairy, audacious goal'. It denotes a strategic and visionary statement that teams are likely to find emotionally compelling.

Would you agree the director made a key mistake here? His unexplained acronym became a business peril. If anyone didn't quite know what it meant, they either would have to:

- put their neck out and ask its meaning; or
- remain in the dark because they didn't dare ask!

Even where you explain an acronym at the outset of a document, it helps to repeat the words in full from time to time. Have you noticed that although I explain the acronym 'non-NE' earlier in this book, I write it in full – 'non-native English' – on many occasions, to help reinforce it for you?

## *Incoterms*

Some abbreviations and acronyms that you are likely to encounter are 'incoterms'. These are commonly used trade terms in international trade. Two common examples are FOB (free on board) and EXW (ex-works).

Do your research on these or other such terms, as using the right standard expressions for each market avoids misunderstandings.

# Active and passive

Most companies today favour the active over the passive voice in business writing, so it's good to understand the difference.

The active voice is where the subject does the action. Sentences that show this are:

The committee took action as a result.

The secretary handed the notes to the director.

The passive voice is where the subject of the active clause becomes secondary, where it is acted upon or receives the action. Often the word 'by' is added, as we can see in the following sentences:

Action was taken by the committee as a result.

The director was given the notes by the secretary.

In both these examples, we can still see the subjects (the committee and the secretary) but they are easier to see in the active sentences, as they appear first. That alone is why it's better practice to use the active voice in business writing. But there are other reasons why active writing is better. The following, very typical, example of passive writing in meetings notes demonstrates this: 'A decision was taken to take the matter further.'

When readers see a sentence such as this, they can be utterly confused. Who took the decision? In operational terms, what happens next? We can't know from the context. We need more information – yet experience shows people often don't go on to ask for that information.

# Nominalization

Many business writers mistakenly think they must embellish or over-complicate their writing! Even the most effective speaker can seem to feel that to write simply and clearly is a sign of weakness.

Sometimes people can't break away from thinking that high word count and complex vocabulary signifies 'we're cleverer than you'. Historically, intellectual, academic writing, for example, uses nominalization, in which nouns are used in place of verbs. This may be useful in writing about concepts. But in business it can seem pompous and outdated. We saw in Chapter 4 how verbs can create vibrant content – and nominalizations do the complete opposite. These examples show the nominalization first, followed by the clearer verb form:

> give clarification on this = clarify this;
>
> in recognition of the fact = recognizing that;
>
> during the installation process = when installing;
>
> we are involved with negotiations = we are negotiating.

The verb form gives more energy: we know that something is happening in each case and that people are involved. With nominalization, users appear to hide behind language. That's rarely a great idea in business.

# Your checklist for action

- Look out for the common confusions described in this chapter. Make a note of others you come across – and ask colleagues too.

- Don't assume readers know the common terms or abbreviations you use (particularly as your writing may be forwarded on to others). Write so that everyone will understand.

- Define the terms you will be using and check that your readers use the same ones.

- Make sure you write plain English, using words precisely.

- Use active rather than passive writing where appropriate.

# Chapter Eleven
# Letter writing

## General

Historically, business letters (now also referred to as 'snail mail') were a formal means of business communication sent by post or courier. In many cases they have either been replaced by informal social media interaction, as we've seen, or by e-mail (or as attachments to e-mail), all mainly for speed. Across the world though, we do still find plenty of occasions where people like or expect to receive a paper letter. This might be for a legal or financial matter, for orders, for apologies for something that's gone wrong, or an invitation of value, and so on.

As you are seeing you can (and must) innovate in business writing today and discard some of the things you may have been taught years ago. Yet there are still certain conventions to follow for your letters to achieve your objectives.

First of all, identify the purpose of your letter and its possible impact on your reader:

- Is it to inform? If so, why?
- Is it to instigate action? If so, what? Who by? How? When by?
- How do you want the reader to feel when reading your letter? Can your tone assist this?

Second, identify the format. Do you use templates and a standard font? Has this been assessed for readability? For example, Arial, Tahoma and Verdana (amongst others) can be more readable than some cursive fonts, especially for non-NE readers. How compatible is the font you use with other systems? Does the font size fall within the routinely used 10–15-point range? Many consider that 12 point offers optimum readability – though you still need to consider the needs of those with visual challenges and other needs, and adapt your writing accordingly.

Do you use a subject heading above your main text? Do you use a reference or code? An informative subject heading engages your reader's attention from the start. It also helps you identify the point of your letter. Customize it if you can. Even the use of the word 'your', as in 'Re: your contract XYZ', is more reader-friendly than 'Re: contract XYZ'. (Incidentally, you don't need to use 'Re:' at all; it's a question of house style.)

Third, identify how well your letters work. Ask yourself questions such as these each time:

- Did I achieve the right result from this letter?
- Or was there a problem? Why was that? Was it because of the English I used? What should I have written?
- Did I get no result when I had expected one? Why was that? Should I use English differently next time I write?

## An example of a letter asking for information

Here is an outline example of writing a letter in English. Even within the UK there are differing conventions as to where to place the date and address on a letter, and what salutations and endings to use, amongst other considerations. Other countries will naturally have differing conventions too. So once again, one size does not fit all and you would need to adapt the outline according to your chosen house style.

**How to set out a business letter in English**

Your company name and contact details
Addressee's name and job title
Addressee's company or organization name
Number or name of building
Name of street or road
Post town
Postcode (UK addresses)
County, district or state
Area code or zip code (US addresses)
Country

Date

Reference number

Opening salutation (with or without a comma, depending on house style)

Heading

Main body of text

Closing salutation (with or without a comma, depending on house style)

Name of writer
Position in organization

Enc. (refers to enclosures, if there are any)

Now let's look at the outline in practice. This is quite a standard letter from one company to another, asking another for some further information regarding a proposed project.

## *Version 1*

This is where the writer does not know the name of the person they are writing to:

---

***The Managing Director***

Trans-Continent Projects Ltd
21–24 Any Street
Anytown
AB3 4CD
UK

16 September 2016

Your reference: RP/01/1220

Dear Sir or Madam
**Your proposed rail projects**

　　We understand that you are launching several rail projects over the next 10 years and are looking for companies who can assist you.
　　As a company with leading expertise in this area, we would be very interested in the concession you propose to award a company for the design and implementation of the necessary railway tracks. For this reason, we would be grateful if you could forward us further details in this connection.

Yours faithfully

Per Smidt
Director
Smidt Holdings

Enc. Please find our company brochure enclosed, as an introduction to our company.

---

Note that 'Yours faithfully' is the traditional UK English convention. In US English you will find such a letter could end with 'Sincerely' or 'Best regards' or 'Yours truly'. Note also that 'Yours faithfully' should be used in UK English only when you do not know the name of the addressee; see below for the convention to observe when you know their name.

## Version 2

If you know the person's name, use it in your opening salutation: for example, 'Dear Mr Smith' (or Mrs Smith, Ms Smith, Miss Smith). This is the formal use of their surname. Or you can write 'Dear Yusuf' (or Sara etc); this is the informal use of their first name. When you end the letter you write 'Yours sincerely' rather than 'Yours faithfully'.

Where possible, try to find out the name of the person to whom you are writing. Naturally, some situations will always stay formal, keeping to the 'Dear sir or madam' formula. But as relationship building can be crucial to business success today, it's really worthwhile personalizing your letter writing.

## Open punctuation

You or your company choose whether you use open punctuation in business letters today. This simply means that you can have a comma after the opening salutation ('Dear ...'), or you can omit it. The same applies to your sign-off ('Yours ...'). Whichever option you choose, be consistent in both the salutation and the sign-off.

# Outline letter confirming a booking

The need to use different styles for different letters is highlighted in the second book in the Better Business English series, *Make an Impact with Your Written English*, described at the end of this book. But this main body of text gives a guideline. I have used a hotel example, as the language of global tourism tends to be predominantly English.

---

Dear Mrs Smith

**We are pleased to confirm your reservation**
Thank you very much for sending us details regarding your proposed stay. We are pleased to confirm the following reservation:

Guest: Mrs Jane Smith
Arrival date: 14 August 2016
Departure date: 16 August 2016
Number of rooms: 1
Room category: double room, non-smoking, first floor
Room rate: summer special as agreed, inc VAT
Reservation number: 007

Your credit card guarantees the room for you.
The room will be ready at 3.00 pm on the day of your arrival and remains at your disposal until 12.00 noon on the day of your departure. It is our policy to charge a 90% cancellation fee for no-show guests, but there is no charge where we receive your cancellation in writing within 24 hours before the date of your arrival.
We look forward to welcoming you to our hotel and hope you will have a very pleasant stay.

Yours sincerely,

Denis Paphides
General Manager
Hotel Beau Rivage

---

Note that in UK English 'ground floor' means the floor of a building at ground level. The first floor means the level (storey) above this. In many countries 'first floor' means the ground floor (US English observes this convention).

## Stay ahead or stay behind

Although you have seen some standard formats, you are also seeing there's rarely just one correct style of writing in English. As circumstances change, we need to adapt and create new designs to work for us and for our readers.

For example, now that companies increasingly deal with customer complaints via social media rather than by letter (as we saw in Chapter 4), companies need to be aware of overly different writing styles within their organization. Look at this Tweet, sent by a train company to a customer (I've anonymized the details) who had tweeted to complain about a delayed train:

TranscountryRail (@TranscountryRail)

@mariexyz I can see you were 11 mins delayed into London Bridge, I do apologise for this Marie. Jon

We see the apology the complainant expects. But the language is still quite formal if we look at it alongside the language used by a fast food chain in reply to a complaint by a customer on Twitter (details anonymized) accompanied by a photo of a newly opened bag of crisps (a UK English word; 'chips' in US and other varieties of English):

Todxyz (@todxyz_)

Are you joking @fastfoodtogo? I was expecting a little more than that when I opened my bag of potato crisps #disappointing

FastFoodToGo (@fastfoodtogo)

@todxyz_ That does look a little stingy! Sorry, did you show our Team Members?

'Stingy' is a colloquial word for 'mean' and denotes 'under-filled' in this context. The informality of social media attunes readers to expect this type of conversational interaction – where companies aren't afraid to express empathy or say sorry where things go wrong.

If the vocabulary and tone in corporate letters is completely different from a company's social media voice, can you see how this can bewilder readers? It can undermine brand consistency – and even credibility. You might 'like' and trust the company's social media voice and 'dislike' even mistrust, a 'formal' letter's distant tone.

Do any of these points strike a particular chord with you or your colleagues? They could make a springboard for wider discussion.

Here's an extract from a letter that continues to impress me over time.

---

Dear Mrs Talbot

**How can I help?**

We value our customers and we make it our duty to understand their needs and requirements so that we can help them to make their businesses work even better.

**Can we do that for you?**

Investing a small amount of your valuable time in a brief appointment is all that I ask of you to enable me to understand your business needs, and offer you helpful suggestions as to how you could reduce costs, at the same time as taking your business forward.

Yours sincerely
Signature and company name

---

The simplicity of the message and the development of a two-way relationship (between me and them) made an impact. This agency achieved this by using creative sub-headings and by writing 'I', 'we' and 'you' – and yes, it worked: I bought from them.

As I said earlier, your English teachers might have said, 'No, you can't write like that at work.' I'm saying, 'Yes, actually, you can!' It can make all the difference between staying ahead in business and staying behind!

# Specific tips about addressing letters

Always check the spelling of the name of the person you're writing to and their correct job title. Readers can be quickly offended when their personal details are incorrect. There may also be commercial implications if compliance-related documentation has wrong details.

It can be difficult, though, if you don't know whether a foreign or unfamiliar name relates to a male or female. Ideally, make enquiries; maybe someone else will know. Or you could use the person's full name at the beginning of the letter – for example, 'Dear Chris Palmer' – to avoid embarrassment or offence.

## *Titles to use when addressing people*

Standard titles used to address people in English are:

Mr (after which you write an adult male's name);

Master (after which you write a male child's name);

Mrs (after which you write a married female's name);

Ms (after which you write the name of an adult female who may or may not be married);

Miss (after which you write the name of a young female child – or an unmarried female, though it's increasingly usual to use Ms now).

Common practice today is to write Mr and Mrs and Ms with open punctuation.

# CVs/résumés and cover letters

Do have a regularly updated CV (also called résumé) as a written overview of your job experience and qualifications, even if you're not applying for another job. It helps you identify milestones you've achieved, the skills you're developing and the personal attributes you have enhanced. It also helps you express 'your brand': what makes you special over and above the next person.

Most CVs are e-mailed to prospective employers, so once again it's your writing that's judged initially. With stiff competition for jobs, employers can hit hard, often ditching CVs with mistakes or that fail to answer the brief or impress.

Employers see a CV as an applicant's 'sales document'. The most articulate speaker in the world might not get to interview stage, simply because his or her written words are the weak link.

So choose words that describe the skills you can bring to the company. Why are you the perfect fit? Research the company and tailor your writing if you want to get the job.

Professional social networking site LinkedIn (amongst others), provides great advice and even CV templates to customize for 'brand you'. They show the current way of doing things, as approaches change. Year on year, they list what they term CV 'buzzwords' that have become clichés through over-use, such as: creative, results-oriented, motivated, responsible and so on. None of them are 'bad' words but if everyone uses them, you won't make your mark.

Showcase how good and impactful your writing style is, and identify the words that list your skills, show your talents for solving problems, improving efficiency, developing relationships etc.

Take time to make your CV 'look good', using all the tips on word power and layout that you've been learning in the Word Power Skills writing system.

As employers increasingly like to hire staff who understand how to write for social media, think about providing links to your online activity, if any, but remember employers will check your posts.

So it's in your interests to show them a professional personal brand. Don't post inappropriate information or discriminatory comments. Reputation matters as much for you as for any company that takes you on.

Include only facts that are true and accurately describe your personal attributes. You must be able to deliver what you say you can.

## Cover letter with CV

Some employers like you to send a good covering letter (or e-mail) with your CV. Use it to improve your chances of getting to interview stage. Customize it and send it with your CV to the correct person, spelling their details and job title correctly, and to the right address.

Once you have correctly addressed your letter, then:

- Show you've done some research on the company and refer to something relevant on its website, such as its values and goals, expressing how yours align.

- Answer the question 'Why should you get the job?' by highlighting the special skills you can bring.

- Don't forget to think of your potential employer (and their likely customers and suppliers), as much as yourself when you write. You've got to persuade and build bridges to get that job!

- Make sure 'brand you' shines out, to set you apart positively from the rest.

- Show what you expect from a prospective employer as much as what they can expect from you.
- State your availability.
- Run a final spellcheck and grammar check; after all, if English is required in the job, make sure yours is perfect in your application! Ask someone's advice if necessary.

Depending on culture and personality, people tend even in their native language either to understate their suitability for any vacancy being advertised or in some cases to over-embellish it. The following non-native English writers' descriptions of their suitability as job candidates definitely fall into the second category:

---

**An accountant:** 'I dispose of untouchable integrity and corresponding success and my brilliance is impressive.'

**A marketing manager:** 'My knowledge, ratio and outstanding attributions decide that my future will be with your company.'

---

These are examples of what I term 'over-Englishing': the desire to outdo native English writers with an exaggerated use of language that deviates from the original. It is in essence an imaginary language – and in the ultimate analysis, it has no meaning! I could rewrite what I think they mean to say (and this isn't at all clear, probably not even in their own minds) as follows:

---

**An accountant:** 'A successful professional with integrity, I will be pleased to use my expertise in the post advertised.'

**A marketing manager:** 'I am looking to take my career to the next level and have every confidence that my excellent credentials, expert knowledge and skills base will deliver what you seek in this post.'

---

# Your checklist for action

- Know how to design a letter well.
- Know what you want the letter to achieve; enable the result you need.
- Understand that the look and feel of your letter needs to align with values shown in other corporate communication.
- Write your recipient's personal details correctly.
- Use the correct salutation and sign-off.
- Edit so readers see your key messages clearly.
- Build in rapport and politeness.
- Represent yourself, your personal brand and your company well.
- Don't make assumptions; write to your brief and for readers' needs. Answer any questions systematically.
- Use spellcheck and grammar check (in the correct variety of English) before sending.
- Don't over-complicate your writing to create impact. It could work against you.
- Design a résumé/CV that will work as a 'sales document' for 'brand you' and demonstrate you have the writing skills that can give you the competitive edge in the information age.
- Keep this updated to show all new skills etc and refresh your style as needed, to avoid clichés.

# Conclusion

**B**y now you will be feeling more confident about writing great English for today's business. You will be closing the skill gap between where you were before you read the book and where you are now – and where you want to be.

There are also two other books in the Better Business English series which follow on from this book to give a comprehensive reference set for your business English writing needs.

## How this series works – and what it is about

The series aligns with the three stages in the business cycle.

My central philosophy is this: writing business English effectively for home and international trade is about creating clear, concise messages and content of value.

### Book 1: How to Write Effective Business English

As you have seen, this book provides effective guidelines and deals with real-life scenarios.

It uses a system that also gives you building blocks to take you to the next level in the cycle of success, set out in Book 2.

### Book 2: Make an Impact with Your Written English

This book takes you a further step forward in your executive career.

There's more on written word power to promote and sell your messages, as well as 'brand you'. PR, presentations, reports, meeting notes, manuals etc are also covered.

## Book 3: Executive Writing Skills for Managers

This book deals with the writing you need at the top of your career and is recommended MBA reading by businesses and colleges across the world.

It gives valuable tips on harmonizing the English that you and your teams use (for example, for evaluation performance). It shows how you don't get to the top by blending in. You have to build bridges, shape outcomes and lead. Your writing needs to make readers buy in to your messages – and keep everyone in the loop.

# This series works with the business cycle

It highlights the essential role business writing plays at every stage in your career, alongside the cycle of business in general. Figures 1 and 2 show how this works. It relates to the three phases this way:

## Phase one: joining an organization or setting up your own business

English business writing needs at the outset of your career: a CV/résumé, e-mail, social media presence, start-up plan, routine business writing tasks.

As you start out, you need to understand how to get the basics right: how spelling, punctuation and grammar and writing correctly matter. You won't get to the next phase in your career – the pitching phase – without getting the basics right.

**FIGURE 1** The business cycle, from the individual's perspective

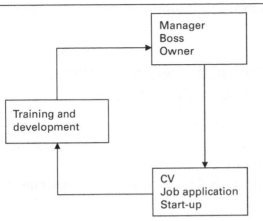

**FIGURE 2** The business cycle, from the business writing perspective

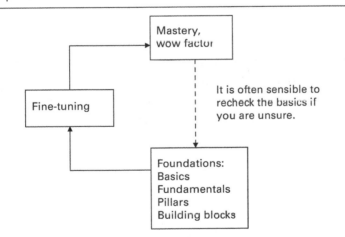

## *Phase two: you develop through knowing how to harness word power*

Your developing English business writing needs: making an impact with everything you write; personal self-development.

Great business English writing generates sparks that capture readers' attention and take your career forward. Powerful writing can sell your proposals so well – weak writing does the opposite.

## *Phase three: mastery of written word power enables you to shine and lead*

English business writing needs at the height of your career: mastery of written word power for leadership, to shine as a manager, boss and/or owner.

You have to build bridges and shape outcomes too.

# The series is an easy, indispensable, comprehensive guide

It's an essential toolkit to keep by your desk or take on your travels. Dip in and out of it as and when you need.

Each of the three books aligns with the business cycle to support your development in writing English for business to gain the competitive edge – because the written word goes hand in hand with, or even is, the business cycle itself.